MANUAL FOR GORILLAS

9 RULES

TO BE THE

"FER-PECT" DICTATOR

First published by Aussie Trading LLC
Copyright © 2019 by Juan Rodulfo
All rights reserved.

No part of this publication may be reproduced, stored, or transmitted in any form or by any means, electronic, mechanical, photocopying, recording, scanning or otherwise without written permission from the publisher. It is illegal to copy this book, publish it on a website, or distribute it by any other means without permission.

Juan Rodulfo has no responsibility for the persistence or accuracy of URLs of external or third-party Internet websites referenced in this publication and does not warrant that the content of such websites is, or will remain, accurate or appropriate.

The names used by companies to distinguish their products are often claimed as trademarks. All trademarks and product names used in this book and on its cover, trade names, service marks, trademarks are trademarks of their respective owners. The publishers and the book are not associated with any products or suppliers mentioned in this book. None of the companies or organizations referenced in the book have endorsed it.

Library of Congress Catalog
Names: Rodulfo, Juan
ISBN: 979-8-3485-4228-3 (e-book)
ISBN: 979-8-3493-0142-1 (paperback)
ISBN: 979-8-3493-0143-8 (hardcover)
First edition
Layout by Juan Rodulfo
Cover art by Guaripete Solutions
Production: Aussie Trading, LLC
books@aussietrading.ltd
Printed in the USA

NOTE TO THIS EDITION: Today April 18, 2025, the United States of America is in the brink of become a neo-nazi dictatorship, pushed by Donald Trump and his fellow billionaire oligarchs.

manualforgorillas.com

manualforgorillas.com

"It is remarkable how easily children and grown-ups adapt to living in a dictatorship organized by lunatics."
A.N. Wilson

PREFACE

When one of my Venezuelan friends or relatives comes to show me, with excitement, the new Military Officer video talking against the Nicolás Maduro Government, I ask them: Who is him or her to decide whether Maduro or Chavez or Diosdado Cabello or Juan Guaidó deserves to be President? If there is a constitution that expressly says that Power resides in the People's Sovereignty[i], nowhere even close says that depends on one or two military that considers the "contrary." When we refer to any country I believe that the State Power must be controlled by civilians, (even though I lost the faith in "States Powers", but this would be the subject of my next book if I keep enjoying the US free speech environment I have had since I fled Venezuela in 2014).

Myanmar calls my attention, and I felt the urgent need to join my voice against the Genocide the Rohingyas people is facing in the hands of the Myanmar's Government Army, but wait, the President Aung San Suu Kyi is the recipient of the Nobel Peace Prize 1991, you may ask yourself: why is she is the Nobel Peace Prize this genocide is happening under his Government?, She is lucky to be alive herself. The military junta, which ruled the country with an iron fist from 1962 until 2011 -- arresting democracy advocates including Suu Kyi, imposing martial law, and killing protestors -- still controls the security forces, the police and key cabinet positions in the government. And there is nothing Suu Kyi can do about it.

"Under the Constitution the commander-in-chief (of Myanmar's Armed Forces) is his own boss, he doesn't report to Aung San Suu Kyi. He cannot be fired," said Aaron Connelly, a research fellow in the East Asia Program at the Lowy Institute in Sydney.

"If the military has to choose between control and international respect, they will choose control. It is a question of how much they are willing to give up. We have not seen much evidence that they are willing to give up anything beyond what they gave up in the 2008 constitution". [ii]

This kind of people, with no respect for other humans with no "military uniform" is the same behind the chair that Hugo Chavez gave in his will to his successor Nicolas Maduro, the same people that earned the Gorilla pejorative adjective in the Argentina of 1955, when that year Argentine Military Officers overthrown Juan Domingo Peron from the Presidency of Argentina, the same Gorillas that stay in power even today, after centuries of Human "Evolution" by hunting, killing and disappearing their political opponents, in this 49 Countries:

Afghanistan, Algeria, Angola, Azerbaijan
Bahrain, Belarus, Brunei, Burundi
Cambodia, Cameroon, Central African Republic, Chad, China, Republic of Congo, Cuba
Equatorial Guinea, Eritrea, Ethiopia
Gabon
Iran, Iraq
Kazakhstan
Laos, Libya
Mauritania
North Korea
Oman
Qatar
Russia, Rwanda
Saudi Arabia, Somalia, South Sudan, Sudan, Swaziland, Syria
Tajikistan, Thailand, Tibet, Turkey, Turkmenistan
United Arab Emirates, Uzbekistan
Venezuela, Vietnam
Western Sahara
Yemen
Zimbabwe[iii]

It is a dramatic nightmare I and my family live every day, we cannot be happy thinking on our Parents, Relatives and Friends suffering in Venezuela, the lack of food, medicines, security, clean water, electric energy, internet, and freedom.

A study by Bertelsmann Stiftung has concluded that a billion more people live under dictatorship now than was the case 15 years ago. The findings were the sum of research for the Bertelsmann Stiftung's "Transformation Index" in which the institute analyzed the quality of democracy, the market economy and leadership in 129 countries.

While the researchers concluded that the number of people living in democracies rose from 4 billion to 4.2 billion between 2003 and 2017, they also found that 3.3 billion people lived under dictatorship last year compared to 2.3 billion in 2003.

The report further warned that growing restrictions on citizens' rights and legal standards were an acute problem in democracies.[iv]

This investigation is based on facts, but in part it is a mockery to the most cowardly kind of people that live on the planet at the expense of the suffering of billions of us. That's why the title says: "fer-pect" instead of "perfect", inspired on the 2004-year Movie "Ferpect Crime" of Alex de la Iglesia, about an ambitious salesman will do anything for that big promotion he's been chasing, but inevitably, he will learn that there is no such thing as the perfect crime. These criminals in power are convinced that they will never face justice for their atrocities, but in the end they all end up like cartoon characters.

Charlie Chaplin – Final speech from The Great Dictator

manualforgorillas.com

My respect and love to all those that suffer the tyranny of this "gorillas."

APOLOGIZE TO THE GORILLAS

I Juan Ramon Rodulfo Moya, human being, publicly recognize you Gorillas as my own ancestors, your DNA and mine is similar from 95 to 99%, you are my next closest relative after the chimpanzees and bonobos, you do not deserve to be compared to these criminals disguised with dark lenses, military uniforms full of shiny colored stuff hanging, surrounded of real military[v] to perform violations of all the Human Rights of the population imprisoned in between the borders of the countries they established their dictatorships.

Gorillas[vi] have a patchy distribution. The range of the two species is separated by the Congo River and its tributaries. The western gorillas live in west central Africa, while the eastern gorillas live in east central Africa. Between the species, and even within the species, gorillas live in a variety of habitats and elevations. Gorilla habitat ranges from mountain forests to swamps. Eastern gorillas inhabit mountain and sub mountain forests between 650 and 4,000 m (2,130 and 13,120 ft) above sea level. Mountain gorillas live in the mountain forests at the higher ends of the elevation range, while eastern lowland gorillas live in sub mountain forests at the lower ends of the elevation range. In addition, eastern lowland gorillas live in mountain bamboo forests, as well as lowland forests ranging from 600–3,308 m (1,969–10,853 ft) in elevation. Western gorillas live in both lowland swamp forests and mountain forests, and elevations ranging from sea level to 1,600 m (5,200 ft). Western lowland gorillas live in swamp and lowland forests ranging up to 1,600 m (5,200 ft), and Cross River gorillas live in low-lying and sub mountain forests ranging from 150–1,600 m (490–5,250 ft).

Gorillas construct nests for daytime and night use. Nests tend to be simple aggregations of branches and leaves about 2 to 5 ft (0.61 to 1.52 m) in diameter and are constructed by individuals. Gorillas, unlike chimpanzees or orangutans, tend to sleep in nests on the ground. The young nest with their mothers, but construct nests after three years of age, initially close to those of their mothers. Gorilla nests are distributed arbitrarily and use of tree species for site and construction appears to be opportunistic. Nest-building by great apes is now considered to be not just animal architecture, but as an important instance of tool use.

Gorillas live in groups called troops. Troops tend to be made of one adult male or silverback, multiple adult females, and their offspring. However, multiple-male troops also exist. A silverback is typically more than 12 years of age and is named for the distinctive patch of silver hair on his back, which comes with maturity. Silverbacks also have large canine teeth that also come with maturity. Both males and females tend to emigrate from their natal groups. For mountain gorillas, females disperse from their natal troops more than males. Mountain gorillas and western lowland gorillas also commonly transfer to second new groups. Gorillas are considered highly intelligent. A few individuals in captivity, such as Koko, have been taught a subset of sign language. Like the other great apes, gorillas can laugh, grieve, have "rich emotional lives", develop strong family bonds, make and use tools, and think about the past and future. Some researchers believe gorillas have spiritual feelings or religious sentiments. They have been shown to have cultures in different areas revolving around different methods of food preparation and will show individual color preferences.

WHAT IS A GORILLA MILITARY

Gorilla is an expression commonly used in Argentine political life to refer to a person who has an anti-Peronist position. The term began to be used in 1955 by the anti-Peronists themselves to call themselves an appreciative sense. Subsequently, the term has also been used by Peronists and non-Peronists, often with derogatory meanings. The expression spread throughout Latin America as a synonym for "right-wing reactionary," militarist, coup-man or "anti-communist."

Origin of the expression in Argentina

In Argentina, the word "gorilla" began to be used in 1955 to refer to an anti-Peronist person. The expression was taken from a humorous painting created by Aldo Cammarota and staged by Délfor Amaranto on the radio program La Revista Dislocada, Carlos Ulanovsky describes that moment saying:

"When the rumors intensified and each gesture was controlled, each movement had a finding: it launched the word gorilla, which was incorporated both in Argentina and in other countries, as synonymous with political, military or civil man, conspirator and reactionary. One hundred times Délfor had to explain that it had all been a coincidence without political intent: at that moment, the film Mogambo, with Clark Gable and Ava Gardner, had been released in the jungle, as the film had had a great impact on the audition. They parodied it. "One of the songs that spread every Sunday "Dislocated Magazine" was a baion, whose lyrics read: "They must be the gorillas, they must be, / they will walk around here, / they must be the gorillas, they should be, / they will walk around there... / The audience interpreted it "as an allusion to what was then circulating with stealth: an underground movement of troops to overthrow Perón".

In 1985, Cammarota told the story in a column written for the Clarín newspaper:

"In March 1955, I made a radio parody of Mogambo (in Dislocated Magazine), a film with Clark Gable and Ava Gardner, which happened in Africa." In the sketch there was a scientist who, in front of every noise in the jungle, said: they must be the gorillas, they must be. "The phrase was adopted by the people. For everything that was heard and happened, the fashion was to repeat" they must be the gorillas, they must be. "First came a failed coup attempt and then the military coup of 1955. The popular ingenuity was left stinging the ball: "they must be the gorillas, they must be." The coup-makers gladly put on that nickname. "

In 1955, shortly before the civic-military coup d'état that overthrew President Perón, spontaneously, the anti-Peronists began to call themselves "gorillas". So did the military anti-Peronist coup supporters of the Navy. In the elections of 1963, the Liberation Revolution Party had as its electoral motto: "Fill the Gorilla Congress."

Once the overthrow of the government of Juan Domingo Perón occurred due to the coup d'état of the self-styled Liberating Revolution of September 16, 1955, the denomination was used to identify the supporters of the new government and, over the years, the term was used by Peronists and not Peronists to name the anti-Peronists, but with a contemptuous sense. By extension, in Latin America began to be called "gorillas" reactionary generals who executed coups, and that exercised a harsh repression against their political opponents.

Later use in Latin America

An example of the use of the term "gorilla" is that made by the Prime Minister of Cuba Fidel Castro in a speech in 1963:

"And what are the imperialists going to do?" They cook in their own sauce and the gorillas take power, of course supported by the United States' gorillas, because in the United States there are also civilian gorillas and military gorillas, the Pentagon's gorillas support the governments of gorillas in military uniform,

and the gorillas of the State Department promote governments of gorillas dressed as civilians, and have their contradictions in there, and those contradictions are manifested in the countries of Latin America." **Fidel Castro**

In Uruguay in the late 1960s and early 1970s, the government of Jorge Pacheco Areco was branded as "gorilla" as a consequence of the systematic application of prompt security measures:

"As of May 1968, great discrepancies between ministers of different origins, such as Alba Roballo, Flores Mora, Queralto, Serrato, Peirano Facio, Frick Davie and Eduardo Jimenez de Arechaga, make the government of Pacheco Areco lose the majority in the Chambers In a complex social and economic moment, the maximum degree was marked by the bank strike that determined the implementation of the Security Measures on June 13 that were constitutionally consecrated for "serious and unforeseen cases of external attack or internal commotion." At 18 de Julio Avenue, they shouted "Gorilla Government, down the measures." The consequence of the measures of June 13 was a new ministerial crisis, Carlos Queraltó, Alba Roballo resigned from his positions and after signing the decree of Prompt Measures of Security, Manuel Flores Mora."

In 1991 the Honduran writer Ramón Amaya Amador wrote the novel Operation

Gorilla, about the coup d'état carried out in that country on October 3, 1963, against the constitutional government of Ramón Villeda Morales with the support of the CIA of the United States. The word "gorilla" in this case is not used in a derogatory sense, but is the name by which the coup leaders, from the United States, identify their own actions against Castro-communism. A paragraph of the novel, in which the American colonel Monkey ("monkey" in English) speaks, says:

"Operation Gorilla" is only one part, very important part of a bigger plan, this you understand, after the power has been consolidated, the second period will come: the military unit of all the countries of the continent, the creation of the inter-American army that be a guarantee of political stability in the hemisphere, in practice, this great multinational army will have the functions of a firefighter: it will extinguish any flame that the Castro-communists ignite throughout the Andes. "

In Venezuela, Antonio García Ponce says in his book Adiós a las Izquierdas that in the 1960s, the left referred to the toughest and most militaristic sector of the government as "the gorilla circle Betancourt-Briceño Linares".

After the overthrow of Honduran President Manuel "Mel" Zelaya on Sunday, June 28, 2009, and his replacement by the then leader of the Congress, Roberto Micheletti, the detractors of the latter began to nickname him "Goriletti", in obvious reference to the term "gorilla" "(Although obviously not as a historical synonym of anti-Peronist, but in general of any supposed or real "right-wing reactionary").

Peruvian President Alan García used the expression on many occasions. For example, in relation to the political crisis in Ecuador in 2010, he said:

> *"IF WE LET THE GORILLAS PASS BY AT THIS MOMENT THE TIME OF THE GORILLA CAN RETURN TO THE CONTINENT."*
> **Alan García, 2010.**[vii]

9 RULES TO BE THE "FER-PECT" GORILLA DICTATOR

"Military dictatorship is born from the power of the gun, and so it undermines the concept of the rule of law and gives birth to a culture of might, a culture of weapons, violence and intolerance."
Benazir Bhutto

RULE 1: Find The "Fer-pect" Place.

The "Fer-pect" place to be a Gorilla is that where you may find plenty of natural resources to sold to Big Corporations or other dictatorships that has not been blocked by the US, the EU or both.

These natural resources may be Oil, Gas, Gems, Coltan, remember something worth to kill millions of people with no remorse!

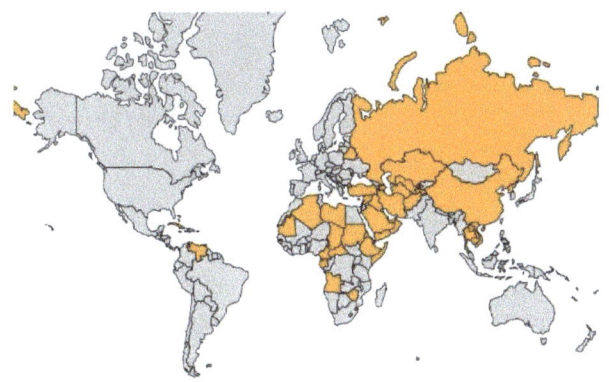

Figure 1 In orange: Countries ruled by dictatorships 2019

Johnny Angel states in his article, published in 2001:

"In the orgy of examination of who and what is to blame for the events of September 11, we must have heard every conceivable explanation. The American right, as exemplified by President Bush, Fox News, and the opinion page of The Wall Street Journal, blames envy of

American values and success. The extreme right blames secular humanism, gay rights, and the other bogeymen they love to flog. The center faults lax airport security and a general lack of preparedness, while the left, all but ignored by the corporate media, blames American imperialism and in some cases our unconditional support for Israel.

Yet for all the noise generated by partisans and centrists alike, no one is willing to accept the blatantly obvious, the underlying factor behind America's involvement in the byzantine labyrinth of Middle East politics. What could possibly motivate the propping up of repressive non-democracies like the Saudi and Kuwaiti royal families, or murderous regimes like that of Reza Pahlavi, Shah of Iran? Or pouring billions into the coffers of Saddam Hussein in the '80s, or even creating the monster that is possibly the mastermind of these attacks, Osama bin Laden, beneficiary of CIA lucre and training?

It is the oil, stupid.

Once again, America's twin addictions, that of its people to cheap gasoline and its corporations to billions of petro-dollars, has led us right into the proverbial pit. Having learned very little or forgotten a lot in the wake of the oil embargoes of the 1970s, America is as strung out on the fossil-fuel jones as any Bonnie Brae Street junkie is on Mexican tar heroin. Even though American dependency on oil from the Middle East has fallen to about 17 percent of national consumption, Saudi Arabia remains the cornerstone, producing 50 percent of the whole world's supply. So, in order to keep this economic balm flowing, to keep the status quo static and the balance sheets of the major oil companies brimming, we have installed our military as a kind of mega police force in the region. Our official reason for being there is to ensure "stability," one of the great buzzwords in the history of business, but this is nothing more than spin -- the military is in the Middle East to guarantee that whatever comes out of the ground is exploitable and controlled by American multinationals. And it is the simple fact of the presence of American soldiers on the holy soil of Islam that has so enraged our new nemesis, bin Laden. Speaking to British journalist Robert Fisk in 1996 Afghanistan, bin Laden made clear his agenda. "When the American troops entered Saudi Arabia [after Iraq's invasion of Kuwait], the land of the two holy places [Mecca and Medina], there was strong protest from the ulema [religious authorities] and from students of the Shariah law all over the country against the interference of American troops," bin Laden told Fisk, who published the comments in The Nation in 1998. The Saudi leaders made a "big mistake," bin Laden said, when they responded by suppressing the protests and cementing ties to the U.S. "After it had insulted and jailed the ulema... the Saudi regime lost its legitimacy," bin Laden said. And so began his deadly fatwa against the United States.

Oil has been the prime mover behind any and every political decision in that region since the First World War, when trucks, tanks and planes replaced horses and camels. Once the internal-combustion engine became the technological centerpiece of the century, keeping it going by any means necessary became a most profitable business venture. And despite the myth that has been rammed down America's psyche for eons, American business loathes competition and aims for monopoly. Sure, they will partner with the Saudi royal family (because the government that they dominate owns all of its oil), but in exchange, anyone in the region who actually believes in the rights of the people of that country to share in the wealth of their homeland is shut out. And forcefully, with the aid of the American military and CIA, as we saw in Iran and during the Gulf War.

This dusty, empty part of the world was basically nothing more than a Bedouin crossroads for 1,300 years, between the end of the Crusades and the early 1900s. During the period when America endured revolution and a civil war, and Europe tore itself apart, the Middle East was downright peaceful. Tell me why the United States and Great Britain reflexively back the state of Israel in its battles with its neighbors. Were it not sitting strategically close to vast pools of viscous crude, no one would give a rat's ass about either side.

It is the meddling in the internal affairs of the Indigenous people of the region to ensure that said oil stays in the hands of the privileged few that has led to an enraged underground movement of terrorists in these lands. And oil is all we are there for -- what else of value comes from that part of the world, what strategic value does it have otherwise?. That may seem as obvious as the nose on our collective face, but it is something no one wants to acknowledge. Especially given the ties between the media and the oil companies: ABC is tied to Texaco, NBC to British Petroleum, Time Warner to Mobil Oil, as revealed in the marvelous media-watchdog flier Censored Alert in the summer of 2000. And now the oil industry is entrenched as America's No. 1 player with Bush and Cheney, two oil men (one failed, one successful) in command."[viii]

A study published in September 2010, by Jesus Crespo Cuaresma, Harald Oberhofer and Paul Raschky, at the Department of Economics of the Monash University of Australia titled: Oil and the Duration of Dictatorships states that:

"The standard political economic model of the behavior of dictators is rather straight forward: The dictator's objective function is the maximization of personal utility via the increase of political rents and subject to the constraint of maintaining political power (Olson 1965, Olson 1991, Tullock 1987). Dictators collect resources from the population and increase personal and family gain as well as amenities of the ruling elite. These inefficient transfer policies are accompanied by a decline in economic development and the degradation of living conditions for at least some groups in society. Sooner or later, unsatisfied citizens might demand a regime change or the deposition of the dictator. Tullock (1987) argues that not all dictators are overthrown, and some might apply a divide-and-conquer strategy to decrease the likelihood of a coup d'etat. Olson (2000) argues that once a dominant "bandit" emerges from a kleptocracy by monopolizing power, he has incentives to limit his theft activities on society and provide some public goods. Excessive theft discourages productive activity and thus reduces future wealth while the provision of public goods enhances income he may exploit for personal gain. Some of the political rents are used to deter citizens from oppositional activities and to ensure that the dictator stays in power. In order to remain in power, a dictator can choose to invest in increasing the base of supporters and/or repression of oppositional groups. Wintrobe (1990) uses the notation of a simple production function with the input factors 'loyalty' and 'repression' and the output 'political survival' to describe the relationship between political survival and the instruments of asserting political power. An increased use of the production factors results in more political power, however, with diminishing returns. Factor prices are assumed to be exogenously given and the factor input is subject to a budget constraint, which basically equals the tax revenue. Although the dictator has a self-interest in setting the tax-rate at a level that does not completely distort incentives for social production (McGuire and Olson 1996, Olson 1993), inefficient policies and possible economic degradation increase the risk of a coup d'etat.

Sala-i-Martin and Subramanian (2003) show how elites used their power to grant import licenses and privileges to cronies and developed a system of corruption that ultimately led to negative effects on long-run growth in Nigeria. A comprehensive overview on the effects of natural resource wealth on institutions and corruption is provided by van der Ploeg (2007). Under the assumptions that most of the rents from natural resources are absorbed by the dictator (e.g. royalties) and that the ruler cannot influence the price of the input factors loyalty and repression, autocratic leaders of countries with a bigger endowment of natural resources have a less constrained budget and may use more of the instruments ensuring their power. Acemoglu, Robinson and Verdier (2004) illustrate how President Mobutou sed rents from natural resources to buy off political competitors. The second strand of literature relates to the ideas of Tullock (1987) that particular dictators (but not necessarily the autocratic regime itself) have an inherent "stability problem".

The key argument is that natural resource endowment can become a 'curse' not just for the overall economy, but also for its ruler. One prominent example is Nigeria, the world's eighth largest oil producer, which has witnessed eight successful coup d'etats between its independence in 1960 and 1993 (Caselli 2006).

This theory combines two different ideas: The first one is that regime change is more driven by private incentives of the challengers or insurgents rather than by the overall social benefit of deposing the dictator (e.g., Grossman 1991). The second one is that natural resources are rents that are more easily appropriated by the ruling elite and thus intensify the rent-seeking contest between various groups in society (Caselli 2006, Hodler 2006). Tornell and Lane (1999) defines this rent-seeking contest as the 'voracity effect'. A recent theoretical paper by Acemoglu, Ticchi and Vindigni (2008) studies the role of the military in non-democratic regimes. In their model the military can act as the dictatorship's tool of repression. However, in cases where the ruling elite insufficiently compensates the generals and soldiers, the army might stage a coup and replace the existing ruling elite with a military dictatorship. Adding natural resources to their model results in two opposing effects for the regime: One the one hand, greater natural resource abundance allows the non-democratic regime to finance repression through the military and thus increases its likelihood to persist. On the other hand, greater natural resource endowment increases the benefits of the army to stage a coup d'etat, install a military dictatorship and thus decreases the survival likelihood of the existing regime. This paper provides a comprehensive empirical analysis on the relationship between natural resource endowment, in particular oil reserves, and dictator duration that combines aspects of both strands of literature. We first present a simple theoretical framework that illustrates the incentives driving the behavior of the dictator and the oppositional group based on the expected benefits from natural resources. Under certain assumptions, a higher endowment of natural resources leads to a lower probability of the oppositional group staging a coup d'etat. Using a dataset on 106 dictators, our empirical analysis supports this prediction.

The theoretical setting is presented in Section 2, and the empirical results are presented in Section 3, Section 4 concludes, but remember: Gorillas do not read too much, nor need to study, if you are not a Gorilla reading this or a civilian learning how to be a Gorilla, you may find the whole study following the link on the reference.[ix]

"Power is not a means, it is an end. One does not establish a dictatorship in order to safeguard a revolution; one makes the revolution in order to establish the dictatorship."

George Orwell

RULE 2: Get yourself a military uniform.

To be the "fer-pect" Gorilla Dictator, you will need dark lenses, not just dark, the darkness you may find in Amazon or eBay, and of course a Military Uniform, full of fancy shiny things hanging everywhere around, with extra pockets to carry extra fancy shiny hanging stars, toys, bullets, tiger teeth, opponents' fingers, etc.

Here you may find some examples:

Figure 2 Haji Hassanal Bolkiah Mu'izzaddin Waddaulah, Sultan of Brunei

Figure 3 Hun Sen, Cambodia Prime Minister

Figure 4 Raul Castro Cuba Ex President

Figure 5 Fidel Castro Cuba Ex-President (1926-2016)

Figure 6 Teodoro Obiang Nguema Mbasogo, Equatorial Guinea President

Figure 7 Muammar Gaddafi (1969-2011),
Libya Ex Prime Minister

Figure 8 Mohamed Ould Abdel Aziz, Mauritania President

Figure 9 Qaboos bin Said al Said, Sultan of Oman

Figure 10 Salva Kiir Mayardit, President of South Sudan

Figure 11 Omar al-Bashir, Sudan President

Figure 12 Prayut Chan-o-cha, Thailand Prime Minister

Figure 13 Gurbanguly Berdimuhamedow, President of Turkmenistan

Figure 14 Brahim Ghali, Western Sahara President

Figure 15 Hugo Chavez (1954-2013), Ex President of Venezuela

Figure 16 Nicolas Maduro, President of Venezuela

Figure 17 Xi Jinping, President of the People's Republic of China

Figure 18 Alexander Lukashenko, President of the Republic of Belarus

If you cannot find this kind of fancy military uniforms, is OK, you may also surround yourself of people wearing them, so, you will look as stronger as the ones with uniform, or you may simply decide to show yourself bare chest riding a horse…

Figure 19 Kim Jong-un, Supreme Leader of North Korea

manualforgorillas.com

"Here in Spain, there are Argentine Jews children and grandchildren of immigrants of Jews who fled Germany or Austria in the thirties, and in the seventies during the dictatorship, they had to go into exile again."
Antonio Muñoz Molina

RULE 3: Learn to yell like a pregnant woman giving birth.

Lair Ribeiro in his book "Magic of Communication" establishes that: "Who knows to communicate has the power," same can happens with our knowledge. Years and years studying with great effort, bunch of books red and homework made, infinite hours in class or the library, long nights studying for tests... And then?.

All this effort would have been time wasted if we did not use our knowledge, which in that case would be like books covered with dust stored in a basement converted into food for termites. Our knowledge, even abstract or practical, is only valuable if we know how to express it to the world. How are they expressed? Through communication. In all ages, since the most remote pre-history, humans have used their communication ability to satisfy their more vital needs. Without communication, our species will not survive. Even to feed ourselves, humans must understand each other and cooperate with others.

This is still valid today. If you like somebody or need something, you need to know how to transmit that feeling. One way or another, you need to share what you know with other people, you need to tell the Universe and transform it into action.

Communication, when carried out properly, transfers power to knowledge and feelings of one person. It means that who knows how to communicate himself has the power: the power to influence, to transform, sensitize, affect, convince, explain, promote great debates, to leave a record of his presence in the world.[x]

But remember, this is applicable to real human leaders, like Mahatma Gandhi, Martin Luther King, Nelson Mandela, Barack Obama, Pepe Mujica, Dalai Lama, John F. Kennedy, Peter Drucker, Noam Chomsky, and several others, you the "Fer- pect" Dictator were sent by God Himself (From the Religion you freely choose), you are directed by the Sun and the Stars, you are above any natural or civil law, you don't need to communicate, since you are the Supreme Entity you are allowed to Yell- Humiliate or even Jail - Kill people around you like Kim Jong Un is doing to his own family and aids, just dispatch orders to your subordinates including millions of people trapped in between the imaginary frontiers of the country you're ruling.

Morgan Meis, in his article: The Dictator's Speech, writes: Some dictators do not know how to talk. They know how to speak, of course. They are able to use language. They utter words, but they do not say anything. Hosni

Mubarak, the current president of Egypt (at least at the time of this writing) recently made a speech in an attempt to quell the street protests and demands for an end to his despotic regime.

You might say it was an airy speech, draped in the finery of general principles, wafting lightly on the breeze of abstraction. He uttered sentences such as, "There is a fine line between freedom and chaos, and I lean toward freedom for the people in expressing their opinions as much as I hold on to the need to maintain Egypt's safety and stability." That is a truly amazing sentence. My favorite part is when Mubarak lets us in on his own deepest feelings and commitments. Mubarak "leans toward" freedom for the people. But wait. He leans toward the freedom of the people only as much as he "holds onto" the need to curtail that freedom in the name of safety and stability. In fact, the sentence ends up denying the very thing it started to affirm. It cancels itself. We know nothing, at the end of the sentence, about what Mubarak intends to do. We do not even really understand where he draws the line between freedom and chaos. He gives no opinion on accusations that he runs a corrupt and despotic regime. The people of Egypt have accused Mubarak of failing them and he responds with thin abstractions about the nature of freedom and chaos. Rarely, in fact, did Mubarak directly address the people of Egypt at all in his speech.

It was a speech ejected over the heads of the people, launched from the room of an interior ministry somewhere, to be immediately filed away in a drawer labeled "Speeches to Suppress Civil Discontent and Remind the People of the Glorious Future, 2011."

The tin ear and woolly mouth of this dictator is rather amusing given the fact that the very word "dictator" comes from the Latin verb "dicere," meaning "to speak." To be a dictator is to be the one who speaks, and the one for whom speaking ought to matter the most. The man in charge is the man who utters the laws, the man who tells people how it is, the man who talks the talk. The dictator speaks and it is the voice of authority. The voice that is, in itself, action. The dictator is the one for whom words and deeds are synonymous. The dictator dictates and the subjects of the dictator take dictation.

When you have a skilled dictator, when the dictator is up to the task, this relationship can work. Life is confusing. Politics are confusing. Wars and natural disasters can leave people without clear direction and with a need for directives. Discussions of the relative merits of democracy aside, the history of human civilization is filled with examples of dictators who really knew how to dictate, for better or worse.[xi]

In March of 2014, was published the study: A Systemic Functional Analysis of

Dictators' Speech: Toward a Move-based Model, by Reza Khany & Zohre Hamzelou in the Procedia Social and Behavioral Sciences Journal, with the following results:

Political genre analysis has for a long time been the focus of attention for many scholars as they supply a rich source of discovery about the nature of language manipulation due to their organized and well-established structure. While politicians may be interested in how to gain support from the public, linguists and critical discourse, analysts might be interested in the way such support is enacted by language. Political language rhetoric has been studied from different perspectives and disciplines such as linguistics, anthropology, psychology, communication science, and discourse science. Much of the impetus behind such studies has been on divulging language misuse and the way such misuse has been legalized. An invisible linguistic misconduct can be attributed to the so-called dictators' speech. Dictators owe their states to words they use to legalize their misdeeds. In order to reveal their disguised intention and disclose their style and structure, this study is an attempt to decipher generic pattern of speeches delivered by some notorious dictators throughout history, Stalin, Gadhafi, and Hitler for instance. Using a Systemic Functional Grammar approach, 20 speeches were rhetorically analyzed which resulted in a move-based model of the genre. The results reported in this study are accompanied by concrete examples along with a mixed method analysis. The findings can be of use both for applied linguists interested in discourse Analysis and language reactionaries interested in the use of critical discourse approaches to the analysis of reading and writing skills.

In order to win favorite responses, everyone is cautious in choosing appropriate sentence structure and vocabulary. In spite of their unique positions, politicians are no exceptions. Speechmakers have a good command of language manipulation skills to persuade the public to accept and support related policies. Dictators are those who mostly benefit from this encoding skill effectively to legalize their government.

The very word "dictator" comes from the Latin verb "dictate," meaning "to speak." To be a dictator is to be the one who speaks, and the one for whom speaking mostly matters. The dictators speak through the voice of authority and by means of language. People listen to them even when they are wrong since language plays the role of a vehicle to end justifications.

From Critical Discourse Analysis point of view, on the other hand, dictator can be defined as: (1) A person who presume himself to be the superpower; so accept no intellectuality, (2) A person who is scared to let people be free and wanted to take control of their lives, and (3) A person who is doing anything but ruling for the sake of ruling.

Since dictators manipulate language to justify their commands, the soul of authority is present within the whole body of their speeches, for instance, by means of mottos or carefully selected structure and vocabulary. By way of illustration, Hitler, one of the belligerent and patriotic notorious characters throughout history, chooses his lexis accordingly (e.g., my comrades, my countrymen) to inject his ideology in a hidden fold. Speechmakers design speech texts meticulously in a way that moves, and sub moves change very gently and smoothly so that there remains a slight degree of overlap between two adjacent moves.[xii]

"When there is oppression and dictatorship, by not speaking out, we lose our dignity."
Asma Jahangir

RULE 4: Do not waste time studying or even reading a book.

The position you are applying for does not need too much effort, I mean intellectual effort, just need as we checked in Chapter 3, a lack of respect for humans and nature, a mental disorder or criminal mind, it's ok you may have one or both, and you will also need after been approved to work as "Fer- pect" Dictator a bunch on friends and guns to show how macho men you are.[xiii]

Dictators are just like the rest of us (at least, at first). If they are not born into powerful families, they will likely need to help their families make extra cash to survive or just make a living on their own until circumstances afford them the chance to take hold of the state's coffers while stomping on the necks of their real and perceived enemies.

Here are the ways a few brutal dictators made ends meet while waiting for their big breaks:

Ho Chi Minh - Baker

The leader of the Vietnamese independence movement that liberated his home country from colonial France, as well as the figurehead for the North Vietnamese who fought the United States during the 1960s and 1970s also brought a brutal form of Communism to Vietnam. 50,000 to 100,000 people are thought to have been killed in his rise to power. He once said: "Anyone who does not follow the line determined by me will be smashed."

Before that, he claimed to be a baker at the Parker House Hotel while living in Boston in the early years of the 20th Century. He also spent time living in New York City, working in a series of menial labor jobs.

Pol Pot - Teacher

Born Saloth Sar, Pol Pot studied a number of disciplines as young man but proved as capable a student as he was a capable leader, which is to say, not at all. He failed as a student in both France and his native Cambodia. When he came back, he taught at a school in the capital of Phnom Penh until he was forced out by the government.

In response, he changed his name to Pol Pot and took charge of the Khmer Rouge, ousting the government and installing himself as leader in 1975. He ruled for four years, presiding over the deaths of a million Cambodians after implementing disastrous economic, agricultural, and cultural reforms.

Luckily for the average Cambodian, Vietnam invaded in 1979 to overthrow the regime.

Adolf Hitler - Artist

The boy who was all set to become a priest dropped out of the seminary in 1903 to become a professional painter. His works were exact, unremarkable, unemotional landscapes that "was ripe for instruction he never received." He moved to Vienna in 1908 and struggled there as a poor artist while the city's culture incubated his racist and anti-Semitic ideas.

He left Vienna to dodge the Austro-Hungarian Empire's draft for World War I. He was deemed unfit for service later anyway. He volunteered in the Bavarian Army as a dispatch runner.

Benito Mussolini - Author

Many dictators penned books. Chairman Mao's Little Red Book is one of the bestselling books of all time. Hitler wrote Mein Kampf. Mussolini wrote romance novels. That is right, romance novels.

The Cardinal's Mistress tells the tragic story of a 17th-century Catholic clergyman and his mistress. Lines like "cast a ray of your light into my darkened soul," do much toward explaining why he was made to take the other fork in the career road, the one marked "dictator."

Than Shwe - Mailman

The man who shipped almost a million Burmese people off to jungle gulags and work camps led one of the most repressive, autocratic regimes in the history of Earth. The military junta led by Than Shwe even executed Buddhist monks by the hundreds, dumping their bodies in the wilds and countryside of Burma.

As a younger man, fresh from school, Than Shwe worked at the Meikhtila Post Office as a postal clerk before enlisting in the Burmese Army and becoming an officer who would later be Prime Minister.

Muammar Qaddafi - Goat Herder

No one knows exactly when Qaddafi was born, but it is widely known his family comes from a Bedouin tribe of nomads who were illiterate and did not maintain birth records. His father was a camel and goat herder who wanted his son to attend school.

Qaddafi would seize power in 1969 while pro-western King Idris was away on state business. Qaddafi increased the Libyan quality of life at the cost of mass political repression and extrajudicial killings. In the early days of the Civil War that would lead to his overthrow and death, he ordered his army to starve the citizens of his own cities and kill any government troops who surrendered to the rebels.

Stalin - Weatherman

Joseph Stalin, the brutal Russian dictator and one of the deadliest dictators in history was actually born Iosif Vissarionovich Dzhugashvili, a Georgian seminary student with webbed toes. He dropped out of the seminary and worked as a meteorological clerk before joining Vladimir Lenin's Bolshevik Movement. He started using the name Stalin around 1912.

The estimated number of people killed by Stalin's regime and its policies range between three and sixty million Soviet citizens, with the higher victim estimates being more common among experts.[xiv]

Fidel Castro - Angry Ballplayer

Persistent rumors would have you believe that old Fidel was a talented baseball player who once tried out for a major-league team in America..., which is completely untrue.

The fact is, Castro did play a little ball back in school: he seems to have been the losing pitcher in a 1946 intramural game between the University of Havana's business and law schools. But the point there is that he was in law school not so much to win ball games as to study law.[xv]

Nicolas Maduro - Bus Driver

He claims that he was Bus Driver at the State Subway Company Metro de Caracas, but people from the company say that never saw him working, but earning a salary as Union Member...

Kim Jong Un - Dictator Son

He is believed to have attended the English- language International School in Gumligen, near Bern, during 1993–98, after which he went to Liebefeld Steinholzli School, Koniz, from 1998– 2000.

He studied at Kim II-Sung University (named after his grandfather), an officer-training college in Pyongyang, from 2002 to 2007.

Even though he had no military experience, he was made a four-star general in 2010, followed by his appointment as the vice-chairman Central Military Commission and his entry into the Central Committee of the Workers' Party.[xvi]

Saddam Hussein - Assassin

In Baghdad, he attended the al-Karh Secondary School and later dropped out. Soon he was introduced to the Ba'ath Party which derives its name from Ba'athism, an Arab nationalist ideology advocating creation of single-party states to end the political pluralism prevalent in the Arabian countries. He was deeply influenced by this ideology and became an active member of the party in 1957.

A plan to assassinate the prime minister was formulated and Saddam was asked to lead the operation. On October 7, 1959, in a bid to slay Qasim, the group started shooting but, due to a serious misjudgment on their part, the prime minister was only wounded. The assassins, however, assumed that Qasim was dead and fled the spot.[xvii]

Anastasio Somoza García - Speak English/Spanish

He was born to wealth and privilege in an elite family with strong commercial and governing experience. His well-heeled family sent the young lad to the United States as a teenager in order to complete his education.

In 1926, Somoza joined an armed rebellion seeking to install his uncle as president of Nicaragua. Although the rebellion failed, the young man gained valuable experience as an interpreter working with negotiators from the United States.[xviii]

Mao Zedong - Assistant librarian

At the age of 11, Zedong attempted to flee away from home to distance himself from Confucian upbringing but in vain. His father soon brought him back. Two years henceforth, Zedong completed his primary education.

Meanwhile, Zedong worked full time in the field along with his father. To satisfy his restless and ambitious mind, Zedong read voraciously. It was during this time that he developed a political consciousness after reading a booklet by Zheng Guanying. The nationalistic spirit of George Washington and Napoleon Bonaparte further propelled his political standing.[xix]

Enver Hoxha - Tobacconist

Defined by Will Nicoll, in his article: Hoxha's pajamas now houses a pro-democracy radio station, as: "a failed French student, one-time language teacher and Tirana tobacconist — has been dead since 11 April 1985."[xx]

Nicolae Ceausescu - Shoemaker

The Romanian dictator was admired, feared, despised – all at the same time.

Today, there are still people living in Romania who think fondly of Ceausescu.

On the other hand, there are those who strongly remember the lack of freedom, the poverty, and the struggle of buying food on a daily basis.

Ceausescu finished only the first four classes of elementary school. He was born in a village called Scornicesti, in Olt County and he had to move to Bucharest when he was only 11 years old.

Then, he became a shoemaker's apprentice and did not continue going to school.[xxi]

Idi Amin - Doughnut Vendor

Idi Amin was one of the evilest dictators in modern history, butchering hundreds of thousands of his own people. And for one young novelist he became an obsession. As the tyrant lies on his death bed, Giles Foden recalls the remarkable life of his tragicomic hero.[xxii]

Josip Broz - Test driver for Daimler

Josip Broz Tito's legacy is a complicated one. After leading a prolific resistance to Nazi occupation during WWII, he ruled a united Yugoslavia for nearly four decades. Tito has been called a benevolent communist dictator, a man who renounced Stalinism, quelled infighting, stabilized the postwar economy, and provided better quality of life for citizens than other Eastern European countries. He also maintained a KGB-Esque secret police force, racked up insurmountable national debt, jailed ethnic pride groups and intellectual contrarians, and perpetrated human rights violations. Hero or tyrant? Ask two Yugoslav expats, and you will get two different answers. Or a punch in the face.[xxiii]

In October of 1910 Josip joined the Union of Metallurgy Workers and the Social-Democratic Party of Croatia and Slovenia and starts taking more active roles in the social and political movements of the time. Taking advantage of unrestricted movement within the Austro- Hungarian empire, Josip took the opportunity to travel around the empire and thus visited Mannheim and Vienna where he employed himself in the Mercedes Benz and

Daimler factory as a test driver of the vehicles between October and November of 1912.[xxiv]

Rafael Trujillo - Telegraph operator

Trujillo was known to treat the Dominican Republic's Haitian migrants with particularly severity and a deliberate disregard for their civil liberties. In 1937, he went as far as to orchestrate the massacre of thousands of Haitian immigrants. When Trujillo was 16 years old, he took a job as a telegraph operator. After joining a gang and committing a string of crimes, Trujillo was arrested for forging a check and subsequently lost his job.[xxv]

WHAT?

There are others that eventually went to College or Universities, reaching their academic goals, like for example:

Bashar al-Asad - Ophthalmologist

A graduate of Damascus University, Asad spent time as a doctor in his father's (Syrian "President" Hafez al-Asad) army. He studied ophthalmology at London's Western Eye Hospital. He returned to Syria when his brother Bassel was killed in a car crash to be groomed to take over for his father as "President" of Syria. Before ascending to leadership, his only administrative role ever, was head of the Syrian Computer Society.[xxvi]

François Duvalier - Doctor

Haiti's 40th president was a democratically elected Black nationalist and classically trained doctor, which made him an excellent butcher of 30,000- 60,000 Haitians. His education also earned him the nickname "Papa Doc."

The 41st President of Haiti was his son, Jean- Claude Duvalier, who was handed the name "Baby Doc," despite not being a doctor at all. Baby Doc fled Haiti after a 1986 rebellion toppled the government.[xxvii]

Mao Zedong read too many books, but none about Human Rights...
YES
Do not worry, most of the Job requires few or no Academic Preparation, just the hungry of power over others and over resources of all kinds, mixed with a strong sense of sadism, mental illness and criminal mind to perpetrate Human Right Violations, Killings and or Tortures, that will keep you in power for a long time.

"Dictators must have enemies. They must have internal enemies to justify their secret police and external enemies to justify their military forces."

Richard Perle

RULE 5 Find the "Fer-pect" Enemy.

Ok, you are now the "Fer-pect" Dictator, and now what? Find yourself some enemies to justify the business bro!

By facing down Nazi Germany, Churchill, de Gaulle, Roosevelt, and Stalin sealed their reputations as great leaders. Legendary warlords such as Alexander the Great, Genghis Khan and Napoleon were military geniuses who expanded their countries' territories through invading their neighbors. Dictatorships feed on wars and other external threats because these justify their existence - swift military action requires a central command-and-control structure.

More than half of 20th-century rulers engaged in battles at some point during their reign, either as aggressors or defenders. Among dictators the proportion rises to 88 per cent. Democratic rulers find this tactic more difficult to adopt because most wars are unpopular with voters. To attract support, the ruler must be perceived as a defender, not a warmonger. The former British prime minister Margaret Thatcher received a lucky boost to her popularity after Argentina, a military dwarf, invaded the British-owned Falkland Islands; she triumphed over her Argentine enemies. Another former British PM, Tony Blair, was not so lucky. Although the 9/11 attacks did much to strengthen his government, his decision to attack Iraq (ostensibly to defend Britain from a long-range missile attack) sullied his legacy.[xxviii]

Internal Scapegoats

Dictators use perceived internal enemies to bolster their cause. Minority groups bear the brunt of the trouble for this perception. By pointing out an internal enemy, the dictator is able to turn the people against his political opposition. Those that support the opposition are therefore cast as enemies of the state.

Caesar's internal enemy was the rich senatorial nobility. As Caesar was a member of the Populares, he cast the Optimates as being out of touch with the populace. He blamed the optimates, somewhat correctly, for policies that had led to multiple civil wars and the unemployment that plagued the lower class.

In Napoleonic France, the internal enemy was the nobility and the Church, but also the rural farmers. At the outbreak of the French Revolution, the nobility was the first casualty. The Church was then targeted because of its riches and ties to the nobility. As the revolution stretched on large scale pogroms were carried out in the countryside to rid France of the rural farmers, who were seen to be supporting the Church. Napoleon consistently cast the return of the nobility as a threat to the safety of the people of France.

In Nazi Germany, Hitler was able to blame the Jews. The Jewish people had cornered the banking market, and some high-profile Jews were connected to the Communist party. Tenuous connections allowed Hitler to provide scant evidence for his oratory and blame the Jews for all the problems of that were facing the Germans.

In the Venezuelan Revolution, the dictatorship blames everybody: the Media, the US Government, the Oligarchy, among others.

External Enemies

Just as important as internal enemies, external enemies form a necessary part of a dictators oratory. After a dictator takes power, he uses the external enemy to unite the people behind a cause. Whether that cause is preemptively attacking, defending, or even just organizing is dependent on the specifics of the situation.

Caesar's external enemies were many, from the barbarian tribes of Germania to the treacherous eastern princes. Of particular note was the Parthian Empire. The Parthians had defeated a Roman Army under Crassus and before his death, Caesar was setting the stage for a grand campaign to avenge that loss. These external threats provided a visceral response from the Roman people that easily allowed Caesar to manipulate the Roman system. With the execution of the Austrian princess, Maria Antoinette, Napoleon did not have to find an external enemy. Austria, Prussia, Great Britain, Spain, the United Provinces, and Piedmont were all trying to invade France to prevent the spread of republicanism. These enemies continued to be a threat to Napoleon's regime, as evinced by the seven wars committed by the Coalitions against France between 1792 and 1815. Hitler's enemies changed along with his fortunes. First on the German agenda was France. After WWI and the punishing Versailles Treaty, Germany had an easy enemy in France. Communist Russia was next on the list and had that succeeded it would have next been Great Britain. By focusing the people outward, Hitler was able to continually extend his mandate to rule without having to end the government formally.[xxix] The capacity of external threats to stimulate internal opposition is a pattern deeply rooted in Russian history. Russia's military confrontation with Britain, France, and Turkey over the Crimea in 1854 brought simmering peasant discontent to the boil and eventually forced the abolition of serfdom in 1861. What Marxist could forget that the uprising of the Parisian communards in 1871 had been sparked by France's defeat by Prussia the previous year?

And what Russian could forget that it was Russia's defeats at the hands of Japan and Germany that set the scene for the insurrections of December 1905, February, and October 1917? Oleg Khlevniuk (1995: 174) has noted: "The complex relationship between war and revolution, which had almost seen the tsarist regime toppled in 1905 and which finally brought its demise in 1917, was a relationship of which Stalin was acutely aware. The lessons of history had to be learnt lest history repeat itself." Soviet leaders read secret police reports of the volatile mood among the peasants and workers before and during the "war scare" of 1927, therefore, with trepidation. At the beginning of 1927 president of the Soviet Republic Kalinin told the Politburo: "I have talked with many peasants and can say straight out that in the event of a conflict with foreign states a significant stratum of peasants will not defend Soviet power with any enthusiasm, and this is also reported in the army." From August 20 of that year an OGPU (security police) report summarizes workers' reactions to the prospect of war (cited by Simonov 1996: 1358): "Kill all the communists and Komsomols [party youth members] who want a war." "If there's a war we'll kill the administration first, then we'll fight." "If you give us war we'll get weapons and make a second revolution." If this was the mood at a time when any prospect of a real war lay far in the future, it was more serious when social tensions deepened further, and the threat of war became still more actual. An OGPU summary dated January 19, 1932, from the time of deepening difficulties over grain sowings and procurements from the new collective farms, claimed the threat of war with Japan had "enlivened 'kulak' activities. In the Moscow region, for example, the kulaks were alleged to assert that 'the kolkhozy are a second serfdom, but we must put up with it for a time, soon Japan will attack Soviet power, and we shall free ourselves" (Davies and Wheatcroft 2003: 15-16). Similar summaries of the popular mood in 1936 reported such remarks as: "Soon there will be war and the Soviet regime will collapse"; "Germany and Japan... will begin the war, and we will help them" (Fitzpatrick 1999: 205).

The idea that internal and external threats may feed each other is not new.

Comparing terror in the French and Russian revolutions, Arno Mayer has described the revolutionaries' belief in the "interpenetration of internal and external counterrevolution." In France as in Russia the terror was, in part, a response to military weakness and external threat. In 1793 Robespierre condemned "the moralists who sought to protect internal enemies 'from the sword of national justice,' insisting that by doing so they 'blunted the bayonets of our soldiers' who were risking their lives fighting the armies of foreign tyrants" (Mayer 2000: 205, 208). In turn, the rise of counter-revolutionary disaffection in the French provinces was often the consequence of the huge military levies ordered by the revolutionary government to fight off the foreign armies gathering to crush it.

An understanding that domestic opposition may be highly responsive to foreign threats is evident in the earliest historical records. In the Peloponnesian wars among the Greeks, for example, it was common for the armies or navies of one side to parade past the cities allied to the other in the hope that the demonstration would provoke a rebellion within the walls, causing the city to change sides. When the Athenians attacked Spartolus in Chalcidice in 429BC they counted on assistance from the democratic faction within the city; on this occasion they were frustrated because the ruling oligarchs called up forces from an allied neighbor that defeated them in battle (Thucydides 2: 79). But the tactic worked often enough that both Athenian expeditions to Sicily, the second of which ruined Athenian power, were raised not to occupy the island militarily but in the expectation that they would weaken the influence of Syracuse, a colony of Athens' enemy Corinth, within the island's other city states, and bring them over to Athens (Thuc. 3: 86; 6: 17).

What Stalin Feared Most: Collusion Among Enemies

Stalin demonized the former oppositionists partly by presenting them as in the pay of foreign powers. Virtually all the victims of the major show trials held in Moscow between 1936 and 1938 were charged with acting in collaboration with or at the direction of foreign governments or intelligence services. The defendants implicated in the "Trotskyite-Zinovievite Terrorist Center" at the Kamenev-Zinov'ev trial (August 19 to 24, 1936) were alleged to have had contacts with the German Gestapo.

The former oppositionists accused of involvement in the "Parallel Center" at the Piatakov trial (January 23 to 30, 1937) were accused of espionage and of trying to provoke a war in which Germany and Japan would defeat the Soviet Union. The Red Army commanders tried in June 1937 were charged specifically with treasonous dealing with Germany, as were many of their subordinates in subsequent processes.

Finally, the defendants of the "Right-Trotskyist Center" at the Bukharin trial (March 2 to 13, 1938) were accused of spying for Britain since 1921 and planning to give away Soviet territory to the British Empire.

Stalin tended to demonize everyone. Davies (1989: 114) has noted that the public discourse of Stalinism relied heavily on the teaching that "He that is not with me is against me" (Luke, 11:23). For present purposes, what is of more importance is that this was not just a rhetorical pose for public consumption but accurately reflected Stalin's worldview expressed, for example, in his private correspondence. Once he had overcome those openly opposed to him and had won unchallenged personal authority over the Soviet state and Bolshevik party, he continued to see the hands of enemies at work in all things. Commenting on mistakes made by the architects of the White Sea Canal on August 27, 1932, he called them "bunglers (or covert enemies)" (Davies et al. 2003: 198); on September 24, 1933, he called those disputing a plan for tractor repairs "bunglers or outright enemies" (Davies et al. 2003: 218). In an earlier incident Soviet trade officials in France and Finland were found to be corrupt; in private correspondence dated September 16, 1931, Stalin described this not as venality but as "betrayal" (Davies et al. 2003: 91). Commenting on the circumstances of the famine of 1932/33 he wrote to the novelist Mikhail Sholokhov on May 6, 1933, that the peasants "were carrying out a 'silent' war against Soviet power. War by starvation" (Stalin to Sholokhov, cited by Davies

1996: 243; in fact, it was predominantly the peasants who were starving).

The previous September at a Central Committee plenum, he heard the speaker declare: "People who can look on cold bloodedly while workers or their families don't get bread for two or three days are degenerates." Stalin interrupted: "They are enemies" (cited by Davies 1996: 257).[xxx]

"Enemy of the People"

Joseph Stalin was a newspaper man, though not quite in the mold of Horace Greeley or Hildy Johnson or Ben Bradlee. When Czar Nicholas II was overthrown in March 1917, Stalin came back from his Siberian banishment and took over as editor of Pravda.

He had to contend with competitive voices in the Russian press for about eight raucous months, until the Bolsheviks seized power on Nov. 7 and Vladimir Lenin established censorship two days later. After that, for Pravda and Stalin, it was clear sailing.

Even after ascending to the pinnacle of Soviet power, Stalin liked to keep his hand in the game. In 1936 he reportedly wrote an unsigned piece for Pravda, headlined "Muddle Instead of Music," about an opera by Dmitri Shostakovich, that nearly drove the composer to suicide.

Just a year later, Pravda took an active role in whipping up the hysteria that led to the show trials of the Great Purge. Now Stalin was not toying with an artist but identifying traitors. To be labeled an "enemy of the people" under Stalin was a death sentence, with execution typically coming only after an abject and wholly fictional confession.

Stalin used the press, unburdened by facts, to create an enclosed atmosphere where paranoid fantasy had to be accepted as reality. He gaslighted his victims, and an entire nation, besides. There was seemingly no way out. (Pravda means truth in Russian, and the name of the other Soviet leading paper, Izvestia, means news; as the old joke had it, there was no truth in Pravda and no news in Izvestia.)[xxxi]

"Stop obeying a dictator; you will then see that he is nothing! Stop obeying a king; you will then see that he is nothing! If you refuse the Devil, you will then see that he will shade away!"
Mehmet Murat ildan

RULE 6: Create or copy a Sticky Slogan, Jingle or Doctrine

On my research to put together the data compiled in this book found that there is a Complete Wikipedia Page[xxxii], dedicated to Political Slogans, indexed from A to Z, I laugh for a while but then realized how easy it has been to convince people around with a simple twitter: 150 Characters, below there are some Dictators' related, and the full list is at the footer:

Catch up and overtake America! (Догнать и перегнать Америку) – Slogan invented by Nikita Khrushchev in 1957 for his vision of the Soviet economy.

Chávez Vive, La Patria Sigue! (Chavez Lives, The Fatherland Continues!) – used in Venezuela after the death of Hugo Chávez to honor his legacy.

Deus, Patria, e Familia – Salazar reactionary slogan Ein Volk, ein Reich, ein Führer ("One people, one empire, one leader") – Nazi Germany.

¡Hasta la victoria siempre! (Until Victory, forever!) – Marxist revolutionary Che Guevara's famous slogan, and how he would end his letters.

Heim ins Reich (Back home into the Reich), describing the Adolf Hitler's initiative to include all areas with ethnic Germans into the

German Reich (Austria, Sudetenland, Danzig,...) that led to World War II.

Me ne frego! – Slogan used by the Benito Mussolini's blackshirts, literally "I don't give a damn".

¡No pasarán! ¡Pasaremos! (They shall not pass! But we will!) – Slogan of International Brigade in Spanish Civil War.

¡No volverán! (They will not come back!) – Slogan of Dictator Hugo Chavez against State Oil Company PDVSA workers fired by himself on National TV Transmission.

Not a step back! (Ни шагу назад!) – The motto representing Joseph Stalin's Order No. 227 issued on July 28, 1942.

Patria o Muerte (Homeland or Death) – A 1960 slogan of Fidel Castro used for the first time at a memorial service for the La Coubre explosion. As a result, it became a motto of the Cuban Revolution and then adopted by the so-called Venezuelan Revolution.

Proletariat of the world, unite! (Пролетарии всех стран, соединяйтесь!) – A Soviet communist slogan coined by Karl Marx from The Communist Manifesto.

Revolution is not a dinner party – A phrase by Mao Zedong, extracted from his full statement that "Revolution is not a dinner party, nor an essay, nor a painting, nor a piece of embroidery; it cannot be advanced softly, gradually, carefully, considerately, respectfully, politely, plainly, and modestly. A revolution is an insurrection, an act of violence by which one class overthrows another."

Serve the People (全心全意为人民服务) – a political slogan of Mao Zedong. The slogan later became popular among the New Left, Red Guard Party, and Black Panther Party, due to their strong Maoist influences.

From each according to his ability, to each according to his need (от каждого по его способности, каждому — по его труду)- Marxist slogan

Tutto nello Stato, niente al di fuori dello Stato, nulla contro lo Stato (Everything in the State, nothing outside the State, nothing against the State) – Early 1930s Italian Fascist slogan.

¡Una, Grande y Libre! – "One, Great and Free!", a Francoist slogan from Spain. It expressed three nationalist concepts; One) indivisible, against regional separatism, Great) in recognition of its imperial past and advocation of future expansion in Africa, Free) not submitted to internationalist foreign influences, which was a reference to what Francoists claimed was a "Judeo- Masonic- International Communist conspiracy" against Spain.

Venceremos (We will overcome/we shall triumph) – A Spanish phrase associated with the Cuban Revolution and socialism in

Latin America and unofficial national anthem of Chile during the period leading up to the coup.

Throughout history, leaders have used or, in some cases, invented an ideology to legitimize their power. In the original chiefdoms like Hawaii the chiefs were both political leaders and priests, who claimed to be communicating with the gods in order to bring about a generous harvest. Conveniently, this ideology often passed as an explanation of why the chief should occupy the role for life, and why the post should pass to the chief's descendants. Accordingly, these chiefdoms spent much time and effort building temples and other religious institutions, to give a formal structure to the chief's power. Henry VIII of England started his own religion when the Pope refused to annul his marriage to Catherine of Aragon. He created the Church of England, appointed himself Supreme Head and granted his own annulment. Other ideologies include personality cults such as Maoism or Stalinism; some serve to unite a nation divided by ethnicity, religion, or language.[xxxiii]

Dictatorship and Ideology

The three big powers in today's world are America, China, and Russia – two autocratic-dictatorial systems and one democracy.

The two dictatorial systems are in some ways different and in some ways similar. Russia maintains a pretense of democracy – Vladimir Putin has just been re-elected president. China has no such pretense – when Xi Jinping was recently re-anointed as party boss and state president there were not even make-believe elections.

They are similar in that both are engaged in aggressive campaigns for domination in their neighborhoods and the wider world, campaigns that aim to undermine the position of the sole democratic super-power and its allies, such as democratic Europe.

They are different in the way they engage for added domination. China is a power with vast resources and is able to make itself stronger by the day. Russia is without similar resources. Its campaign is therefore one of strategic relativism. Says Timothy Snyder in his just published The Road to Unfreedom: "Russia cannot become stronger, so it must make others weaker." This difference also makes for campaigns different in character. China is an elegant player on the world stage. Russia is an ugly and thuggish player.

Both engage, in their different ways, with assertive determination. This assertiveness and determination come from both states being ideological states. In both countries, the leaders have dressed up their systems in similar ideological cloaks. They are now both nationalistic powers.

Putin's Russia, explains Timothy Snyder, is inspired by a vision of a greater Russian spiritual empire. This explains, for example, Russia's aggression in the Ukraine, a country that cannot be democratic and European because it is part of spiritual Russia. China is inspired by Xi Jinping's "China Dream" of China's "great national rejuvenation." This explains, for example, China is building of a new global architecture of power in the "Belt and Road Initiative" with the aim of China reclaiming its global position as "the middle kingdom."

Both nationalistic narratives are also narratives of state and society. In both cases, the unity of purpose is the nation. The core of this thinking is that the nation is one and indivisible and that individuals have their existence as components of the nation. In the Russian case, which Snyder characterizes as no-nonsense neo-fascism, individualism is seen to be the idea of European decadence. European democracy, and the European Union, are therefore the enemies of spiritual Russia, not because of what they do but because of what they are. In the Chinese case, the "Dream" contains not only a vision of national greatness but also the idea, in Xi's words at the launch of the "Dream," that "each person's future and destiny is closely linked with the future and destiny of the country and nation." Nationalistic ideology gives both these powers backing for aggressive assertiveness, all the more being ideologies that submerge individuals into the nation. There is then no autonomous good for individuals that stands in the way of the good of the nation, nor of the state that is the custodian of the national good.

Democratic countries are by definition non- ideological. That is their strength in terms of value. The idea that the state is the servant of the person is morally superior to the idea that it is the servant of the nation in the meaning that people do not matter.

In power terms, are non-ideological democratic regimes at a disadvantage vis-à-vis ideological autocratic regime? That is probably not the experience, but they may be at a disadvantage in some ways. It may be difficult from a democratic vantage point to grasp and understand the nature of ideologically motivated autocratic assertiveness. That seems to be the case today. The West appears unable to make sense of Putin's Russia and Russian policies of aggression in the Ukraine and Syria, and of destabilization in Europe and America. The West also appears unable to make sense of Xi's China and China's audacious design towards no less than a new world order. The West is hopelessly lacking in hard-nosed realism up against very hard-nosed aggression from the autocratic powers.[xxxiv]

"It is true you cannot eat freedom, and you cannot power machinery with democracy. But then neither can political prisoners turn on the light in the cells of a dictatorship."
Corazón Aquino

RULE 7: Have fun sending people to Jail, Killing or Disappearing the Opposition

Get rid of your political enemies or, more cleverly, embrace them in the hope that the bear hug will neutralize them. Zimbabwe's former dictator Mugabe abandoned the unpopular practice of murdering political rivals and instead bribed them, with political office, for their support. Idi Amin, who came to power in Uganda after a military coup, stuck with the murderous route: During his eight years at the top, he is estimated to have killed between 80,000 and 300,000 people. His victims included cabinet ministers, judicial figures, bankers, intellectuals, journalists, and a former prime minister. At the lower end of the scale, which is a hit rate of twenty-seven executions a day.[xxxv]

Sergei Guriev and Daniel Treisman, in their study titled: How Modern Dictators Survive: An Informational Theory of the New Authoritarianism, published in November 2015, found scientific answers to the Question: How do dictators hold onto power? The totalitarian tyrannies of Stalin, Hitler, Mao, Pol Pot, and others relied largely although not exclusively on mass terror and indoctrination. Although less ideological, many 20th Century military regimes—from Franco's Spain to Pinochet's

Chile—used considerable violence to intimidate opponents of the regime. Personalistic dictators in Africa and the Caribbean—such as Mobutu, Bokassa, Somoza, and the Duvalier's—also relied on blood and fear to sustain their rule. However, in recent decades, a less carnivorous form of authoritarian government has emerged, one better adapted to the globalized media and sophisticated technologies of the 21st Century. From the Peru of Alberto Fujimori to the Hungary of Viktor Orban, illiberal regimes have managed to consolidate power without isolating their countries from the world economy or resorting to mass killings.

    Instead of inaugurating "new orders," such regimes simulate democracy, holding elections that they make sure to win, bribing and censoring the private press rather than abolishing it, and replacing ideology with an amorphous anti-Western resentment. Their leaders often enjoy genuine popularity—albeit after eliminating plausible rivals that is based on "performance legitimacy," a perceived competence at securing prosperity and defending the nation against external or internal threats. State propaganda aims not to re-engineer human souls but to boost the leader's ratings, which, so long as they remain high, are widely publicized.

Political opponents are harassed and humiliated, accused of fabricated crimes, and encouraged to emigrate.

The new-style dictators can brutally crush separatist rebellions and deploy paramilitaries against unarmed protesters. But, compared to most previous autocrats, they use violence sparingly. They prefer the ankle bracelet to the Gulag. Maintaining power, for them, is less a matter of terrorizing victims than of manipulating beliefs about the world. Of course, totalitarian leaders also sought to influence public beliefs some were great innovators in the use of propaganda. Yet, how they used it was quite different. Dictators such as Hitler and Stalin sought to fundamentally reshape citizens' world views by imposing comprehensive ideologies. The new autocrats are more surgical: they aim only to convince citizens of their competence to govern. The totalitarian dictators often employed propaganda to encourage personal sacrifices for the "common good." Their successors seek to manipulate citizens into supporting the regime for selfish reasons.

Finally, although propaganda was important for the old-style autocracies, violence clearly came first. "Words are fine things, but muskets are even better," Mussolini quipped (Odegard 1935, p.261). Recent tyrannies reverse the order. "We live on information," Fujimori's security chief Vladimiro Montesinos confessed in one interview. "The addiction to information is like an addiction to drugs." Montesinos paid million-dollar bribes to television stations to skew their coverage. But killing members of the elite struck him as foolish: "Remember why Pinochet had his problems. We will not be so clumsy" (McMillan and Zoido 2004, p.74).

When dictators are accused of political murders these days, it often augurs the fall of the dictatorship. Some bloody military regimes and totalitarian states remain for instance, in Egypt and Burma, or North Korea. And some less violent non- democracies existed even in the heyday of authoritarian repression (mostly monarchies and post-colonial African regimes). But the balance has shifted. Compared to 35 years ago, far more of the undemocratic orders around today have elected legislatures in which nongovernment parties occupy a significant place. And fewer are currently involved in mass atrocities against their populations. Whereas in 1975 22 percent of non-democracies were engaged in mass killings, by 2012 this share had fallen to 6 percent. Besides Fujimori's Peru and Orban's Hungary, other regimes that share some or all of these characteristics include Vladimir Putin's Russia, Mahathir Mohamad's Malaysia, Hugo Chavez's Venezuela, and Recep Tayyip Erdogan's Turkey. One might even see Lee Kuan Yew's Singapore as a pioneer of such "soft autocracy." China's recent party bosses also fit in some respects, but whereas the other leaders inherited flawed democracies and undermined them further, the institutions hollowed out in China were those of totalitarian

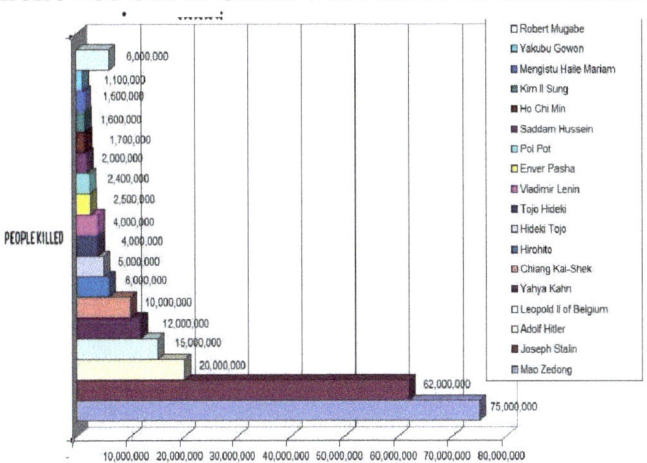

"I have often thought that if a rational Fascist dictatorship were to exist, then it would choose the American System."

Noam Chomsky

RULE 8: Free Media? Jail'em All and create your own.

One of the first actions of any aspiring dictator should be to control the free flow of information, because it plugs a potential channel of criticism. Turn the media into a propaganda machine for your regime like Hitler did and Erdogan does now. Other leaders, such as Myanmar's ruling junta, shut down media outlets completely. Democratically elected leaders are somewhat more restrained, but if they have enough powers they can rig an election or do away with meddlesome journalists (like Vladimir Putin's Russia) or, if money is no object, build their own media empire. Former Italian Prime Minister Silvio Berlusconi owned nearly half the Italian media, encompassing national television channels, radio stations, newspapers, and magazines. Unsurprisingly, these outlets carefully managed Berlusconi's public image and shielded him from criticism. Aspiring dictators should note that muzzling the media is most effective in an ordered society: a 2007 poll of more than 11,000 people in fourteen countries, on behalf of the BBC, found that 40 per cent of respondents across countries from India to Finland thought social harmony more important than press freedom.[xxxvii]

Sergei Guriev and Daniel Treisman[xxxviii], in their study titled: How Modern Dictators Survive: An Informational Theory of the New Authoritarianism, published in November 2015, developed a model of dictatorship to capture the logic that governs the survival of such regimes. As in signaling models of democratic politics, the ruler may be either competent or incompetent. Only the dictator and a subset of the public — "the informed elite"— observe his type directly. But ordinary citizens update their beliefs about this based on the information available to them from the state media, independent media, and their own living standards. Citizens' private consumption depends on the tax rate set by the dictator and on economic performance, itself a function of the leader's competence and a stochastic shock.

If enough citizens infer, based on these various signals, that the incumbent is incompetent, they overthrow him in a revolution. Members of the elite —if not co-opted— would also prefer to replace an incompetent incumbent but cannot do so without the masses to back them up.

The dictator can affect all the channels of information. He can spend on making the propaganda broadcast via state media more convincing. He can bribe (or impose costs—such as fines or violence—on) the informed elite to prevent the latter from sending critical messages. And he can censor those messages that they do send.

The dictator can also spend on hiring and equipping the police with the tools of repression, thus increasing the cost of revolution. However, all these actions must be paid for by the government, either by raising the tax rate (which reduces after- tax income and therefore consumption for citizens) or by reducing government spending on other items, which may include public services that the population values. Policemen assigned to intimidate journalists are not solving real crimes. Citizens, observing their lower consumption or the depleted supply of public services, will downgrade their estimates of the incumbent's competence. Hence the tradeoff.

"Propaganda" here should be understood broadly: it refers to any action by the government that makes the message "the leader is competent" more convincing to the public. Thus, it includes traditional instruments such as government advertising, production and broadcast of distorted news shows, pro-regime online media, bribing and planting of stories in the supposedly independent press, and hiring of internet "trolls" to post pro- regime comments. In China, an estimated 20 percent of all internet comments come from members of the "50 cent party," so-called because of the fee each is paid per pro-government post (Simon 2015, p.99).

In addition, reforming school curricula to make them more "patriotic" may fit (Cantoni et al., 2014). But propaganda can also be understood to include actions of the government that render credible the leader's excuses for poor economic performance.

These could include manufacturing diplomatic, economic, and even military confrontations with foreign powers so that they can be more convincingly blamed for domestic stagnation. Of course, such actions can be very costly for the country but still rational for the dictator if the propaganda benefit is large.

Censorship, in the new dictatorships, also involves a mix of traditional and non-traditional methods. Besides blocking publication of specific articles or programs, it can include filtering the internet, hiring hackers to attack opposition websites, bribing the owners and journalists in "independent" media to censor themselves, and prosecuting and imprisoning journalists who refuse. It can also involve paying friendly investors to buy out and domesticate critical broadcasters, overtly or through shell companies. Such activities divert resources from productive uses and cut into government spending on welfare-enhancing programs.

China reportedly employs two million censors to police the internet (Bennett and Naim 2015). Under Fujimori in Peru, the regime paid more than $36 million a year to the main television channels to skew their coverage and reportedly offered one channel a $19 million bribe (McMillan and Zoido 2004, pp.82-5).

They identify two stable equilibria: in one the dictator co-opts the elite, in the other he censors the private media. Multiple equilibria exist because members of the elite must coordinate on a strategy. When both equilibria exist, the one with co-optation always yields the dictator higher survival odds than the one with censorship. They also find that, so long as force is not too cost-effective, it is used against the general public only as a last resort after co-optation, censorship, and propaganda have failed.

Repression is not necessary if mass beliefs can be manipulated sufficiently by means of censorship, co-optation, and propaganda. Indeed, since in their model major repression is only used if equilibria based on co-optation and censorship have disappeared, violence signals to the general public that the regime is incompetent and therefore vulnerable. For instance, the appearance in 2000 of a tape that seemed to implicate Ukrainian President Leonid Kuchma in the killing of a journalist set off protests that led ultimately to the country's "Orange Revolution" four years later. Conversely, when co-optation and censorship have failed an opposition to the regime becomes overt, state repression is all that remains and is sure to be used.

As Davenport (2007, pp.7-8) notes, one result that emerges with "astonishing consistency" from studies of repression is that: "When challenges to the status quo take place, authorities generally employ some form of repressive action to counter or eliminate the behavioral threat."

Second, the effectiveness of propaganda in authoritarian regimes is a prima facie puzzle. Given that citizens know the dictator has an incentive to lie about his type, why do they ever listen? In their model, propaganda works because whereas competent leaders can costless show themselves to be competent, incompetent ones must invest resources to fake the evidence that will make this claim convincing and sometimes they choose to spend their budget on other actions instead. Thus, observing a dictator claim persuasively to be competent increases the odds that he actually is— especially given the resources he could shift from propaganda to consumption and public goods which are directly observed by the public.

Third, the model offers one reason some clearly incompetent dictators nevertheless manage to retain power for long periods. Rulers whom most or all citizens —if fully informed— would prefer to overthrow can still survive in many circumstances simply by manipulating information.

Moreover, they show that over time incompetent leaders, if they survive, may acquire a reputation for competence as a result of rational Bayesian updating by citizens. Such reputations can withstand temporary economic downturns if these are not too large. This is consistent with the empirical finding that dictators that last through their first few years are less likely to be overthrown (Svolik 2009, Bueno de Mesquita and Smith 2010, Treisman 2014).

Fourth, the multiple equilibria associated with different leader strategies illuminate why, among dictatorships that seem otherwise quite similar, some focus on censoring independent media while others censor much less but co-opt the elite with patronage. For example, while Iran has the world's strictest limits on internet content, according to Freedom House, Morocco has among the least restrictive internet controls, on a par with those of Japan (Freedom House 2013). The Moroccan royal family has consistently viewed co-optation "as a much more effective tool than confrontation and repression," given the country's traditional system in which "patronage and accommodation were deeply ingrained" (Willis 2014, p.444).

Fifth, the model predicts that as economic conditions worsen a dictatorship may boost relative spending on censorship and propaganda. This is consistent with a noted increase since the global financial crisis in efforts to limit opposition media in a range of countries, from Hungary and Turkey to Russia. For example, as Turkey's growth rate fell from 7.8 percent in 2010 to 0.8 percent in 2012, according to the World Bank, the number of journalists in jail increased from 4 to 49.5 Between 2008 and 2011, Hungary fell fifteen percentage points on Freedom House's press freedom index. Conversely, China, while certainly not eschewing censorship, seems to have placed an increasing focus on consumption and provision of public goods during its long period of rapid growth. Starting in the 1980s, Beijing replaced the Mao-era system of comprehensive control with one that relied increasingly on co-optation and commercialized self-censorship; media owners, editors, and journalists are rewarded for loyalty with state advertising contracts and well-paid jobs, thus incentivizing them to censor themselves. "The desire to win performance bonuses tends to result in journalism that steers well clear of dangerous political controversy and meets the party's propaganda requirements," according to one analyst (Esarey 2005, pp.57-9). Censorship of the internet, meanwhile, has focused on blocking collective action rather than on suppressing criticism of the government and party (King, Pan, and Roberts 2013). In Singapore as well, "forsaken profits and stiff legal penalties have been more effective in fostering self-censorship than earlier methods of intimidation" (Rodan 1998, p.69).

Sixth, the model offers a variety of reasons why—as widely noted—modernization makes dictatorship harder to sustain, at least in the absence of vast resource rents. By increasing the size of the "informed elite," economic development increases the cost for incompetent dictators of either co- opting potential critics or censoring their media messages. Even relatively small economic shocks then become sufficient to threaten the incumbent's rule. If modernization also increases the technological sophistication of opposition media, then censorship may fail for this reason as well.

Yet, if modernization makes it harder to sustain an information-based dictatorship, we believe it increases the costs of mass repression even more. An autocrat's greatest nightmare is that his security services, when ordered to violently suppress opposition, will split, or simply disobey, igniting a power struggle that undermines the regime (Francisco 2005, p.66). The more educated, globally integrated, and professionalized are the dictator's agents, the greater is the chance they will shrink from committing a massacre. At the same time, harsh repression is both more public and more economically harmful in a more developed society. A knowledge economy, dependent on innovation, stands to lose its entrepreneurs to emigration if the dictator uses force. In a world of global media and capital flows, political violence can depress foreign investment, stimulate capital flight, and even puncture confidence in the currency (Blanton and Blanton, 2007, Fielding and Shortland, 2005). All these factors help explain the modern dictator's preference for less overt methods.

The International Forum for Democratic Studies in their website: "Resurgent Dictatorship", established that:

"Authoritarian governments employ state-run and state-friendly media to create and control domestic political narratives. Designed to appeal to wide audiences with entertainment content, these media outlets make potent weapons for tarnishing political opposition and civil society activists while discrediting protest movements at home and abroad as harbingers of chaos. As a rule, government programs receive privileged access to the airwaves. The presidents of Ecuador and Venezuela routinely appear on their own, lengthy talk shows or on mandatory broadcasts to denounce political opposition, and Russian President Vladimir Putin is similarly famous for his hours-long telethons. Meanwhile, resource constraints, legal pressure, and other restrictions often keep dissenting voices out of the news altogether.

Beyond their borders, authoritarian regimes distort political narratives through significant investments in international broadcasting. Russia's international television broadcaster, RT, is known for fabricating news stories, misrepresenting interviewees, and airing testimony from fake experts. RT and its Internet and radio counterpart, Sputnik, have become key instruments in the Kremlin's information war against Ukraine. In the Middle East, Saudi Arabia's international broadcaster, Al Arabiya, competed fiercely with Al Jazeera to shape political narratives in Egypt during the administration of former President Mohammed Morsi. In Africa, China's growing investments in the media sector through China Central Television (CCTV) and other outlets gives the Chinese Communist Party editorial line the opportunity to influence audiences far from Beijing.

Authoritarian leaders understand the power of ideas and seek to limit criticism at home and abroad by subverting traditional sources of thought leadership and injecting their own narrative into the information space. While state- owned international broadcasting outlets play a key role, other institutions are also involved. For example, China's Confucius

Institutes undermine academic freedom by limiting criticism of key issues the Chinese government deems to be sensitive. China, and other repressive governments, has systematically placed in international publications polished advertising supplements, such as China Watch. Russia similarly funds websites, newsletters, and other non-broadcast sources to target international audiences. Some analysts suggest this strategy is less about presenting observers with a coherent counter narrative than with sowing confusion, apathy, and cynicism abroad as a cover for deepening authoritarianism and escalating aggression.

Many of these opaque organizations feature analysts of unknown origin, and some may not exist at all. The work of these "fake think tanks" is often plagiarized or fabricated, and it is disseminated by a legion of state-funded Internet bots and trolls. China and other authoritarian states have deployed such troll accounts domestically to bully online dissidents and shut down debate. When these tactics are insufficient, authoritarian regimes may enlist Western bloggers, public relations firms, and lobbyists to make their cases for them." [xxxix]

The Journalist Eladio Rodulfo Gonzalez (My Father), published in 2018 a couple of researches titled: "La Guerra Asimétrica del Dictador Hugo Chávez contra Comunicadores Sociales y Medios" (The Asymmetric War of

Dictator Hugo Chavez against Journalists and Media) and "La Guerra Asimétrica del Dictador Nicolás Maduro contra Comunicadores Sociales y Medios" (The Asymmetric War of Dictator Nicolas Maduro against Journalists and Media), both in different releases starting on year 2004 until 2018, a compilation of Press Releases on how the Dictatorship since it beginnings started a fierce campaign of persecution against Journalists and Media Outlets National and Foreigners, including in sometimes jail and assassinations.[xl]

LA GUERRA DEL DICTADOR
HUGO CHAVEZ
CONTRA COMUNICADORES SOCIALES Y MEDIOS

2004

Rodulfo Gonzalez
Estado Nueva Esparta, Venezuela, Septiembre 2018

manualforgorillas.com

"It has been claimed at times that our modern age of technology facilities dictatorship."
Henry A. Wallace

RULE 9: Update your Business.

This is XXI Century my man!, It is time to update your Business!. You cannot be the "Fer-pect" Dictator anymore if you do not censor Social Media, Internet or Troll it away or even use Hip- Hop to convince people that you are a nice guy... Governments worldwide are stepping up their use of online tools, in many cases inspired by China's model, to suppress dissent and tighten their grip on power, a human rights watchdog study found Thursday.

The annual Freedom House study of sixty-five countries found global internet freedom declined for the eighth consecutive year in 2018, amid a rise in what the group called "digital authoritarianism." The Freedom on the Net 2018 report found online propaganda and disinformation have increasingly "poisoned" the digital space, while the unbridled collection of personal data is infringing on privacy. "Democracies are struggling in the digital age, while China is exporting its model of censorship and surveillance to control information both inside and outside its borders," said Michael Abramowitz, president of Freedom House.

"This pattern poses a threat to the open internet and endangers prospects for greater democracy worldwide." Chinese officials have held sessions on controlling information with thirty-six of the sixty-five countries assessed and provided telecom and surveillance equipment to a number of foreign governments, Freedom House said. The report found seventeen governments approved or proposed laws restricting online media in the name of fighting "fake news," while eighteen countries increased surveillance or weakened encryption protection to monitor their citizenry more closely. According to the researchers, internet freedom declined in twenty-six countries from June 2017 to May 2018. Gains were seen in nineteen countries, most of them minor.

China's 'techno-dystopia'

One of the greatest threats, Freedom House said, is efforts by China to remake the digital world in its "techno-dystopian" image.

It cited a sweeping Chinese cybersecurity that requires that local and foreign companies "immediately stop transmission" of banned content and compels them to ensure that data on Chinese users is hosted within the country. This has been followed by "hundreds" of new directives on what people can and cannot do online, and tighter controls on the use of VPNs to evade detection. The report said leaked documents and other evidence suggest as many as a million Muslims may be held in internment camps in Xinjiang, many as a result of nonviolent online activities. China appears to be using its big tech firms involved in telecom infrastructure to extend its dominance and gain an edge in surveillance, according to Freedom House. Companies such as Huawei – largely banned from contracts in the US and Australia – are building infrastructure in many parts of the world including Africa and Latin America, according to Freedom House board chairman Michael Chertoff, a former US secretary of homeland security. "This opens up a potential for exploiting information in these countries by having technological backdoors that can be used by the Chinese government to collect intelligence," Chertoff told a conference call.

Suppressing dissent

The researchers said online freedom is facing threats in democratic as well as authoritarian states. India led the world in the number of internet shutdowns, with over one hundred reported incidents in 2018 so far, claiming that the moves were needed to halt the flow of disinformation and incitement to violence.

Similar actions were taken in Sri Lanka and elsewhere.

"Cutting off internet service is a draconian response, particularly at a time when citizens may need it the most, whether to dispel rumors, check in with loved ones, or avoid dangerous areas," Freedom House researcher Adrian Shahbaz said. "While deliberately falsified content is a genuine problem, some governments are increasingly using 'fake news' as a pretense to consolidate their control over information and suppress dissent." Shahbaz said more governments, including Saudi Arabia, are employing "troll armies" to manipulate social media and in many cases drown out the voices of dissidents. "It has now become a tool of authoritarian diplomacy to deploy an army of electronic trolls," he said. The researchers said online freedom also declined in the United States in part due to the rollback of "net neutrality" rules which ensured that all data be treated equally, without "fast" or "slow" lanes for commercial or other reasons. It said online freedom also faces threats in the US as a result of the reauthorization of a surveillance law and a "hyper partisan" environment in social media marked by large disinformation efforts.[xli]

Richard Fontaine & Kara Frederick published, a couple of weeks ago (March 15, 2019), on the Wall Street Journal their research named: "The Autocrat's New Tool Kit", that goes like this:

"As dystopian and repressive as these efforts sound, just wait. They may soon look like the quaint tactics of yesteryear. A sophisticated new set of technological tools—some of them now maturing, others poised to emerge over the coming decade—seem destined to wind up in the hands of autocrats around the world. They will allow strongmen and police states to bolster their internal grip, undermine basic rights and spread illiberal practices beyond their own borders. China and Russia are poised to take advantage of this new suite of products and capabilities, but they will soon be available for export, so that even second-tier tyrannies will be able to better monitor and mislead their populations.

Many of these advances will give autocrats new ways to spread propaganda, both internally and externally. One key technology is automated microtargeting. Today's microtargeting relies on personality assessments to tailor content to segments of a population, based on their psychological, demographic or behavioral characteristics. Russia's Internet Research Agency reportedly conducted this kind of research during the 2016 U.S. presidential race, harvesting data from Facebook to craft specific messages for individual voters based in part on race, ethnicity and identity. The more powerful microtargeting is, the easier it will be for autocracies to influence speech and thought.

Until now, such efforts have been mostly limited to the commercial world and have focused on precision advertising: Facebook itself conducts microtargeting, for instance, and Google labeled users "left-leaning" or "right-leaning" for political advertisers in the 2016 election. But private firms are developing artificial intelligence that can automate this customization for whole populations, and government interest is sure to follow. In an October 2018 discussion at the Council on Foreign Relations, Jason Matheny, the former director of the U.S. government's Intelligence Advanced Research Projects Activity, cited this kind of "industrialization of propaganda" as one reason to beware of the "exuberance in China and Russia towards AI."

"CHINA IS THE LEADER IN DEVELOPING NEW FORMS OF CONTROL AND IS EAGER TO EXPORT THEM."

AI-driven applications will soon allow authoritarians to analyze patterns in a population's online activity, identify those most susceptible to a particular message and target them more precisely with propaganda. In a widely viewed TED Talk in 2017, techno-sociologist Zeynep Tufekci described a world where "people in power [use] these algorithms to quietly watch us, to judge us and to nudge us, to predict and identify the troublemakers and the rebels." The result, she suggests, may be an authoritarianism that transforms our private screens into "persuasion architectures at scale...to manipulate individuals one by one, using their personal, individual weaknesses and vulnerabilities." This is likely to mean far more effective "influence campaigns," aimed at either citizens of authoritarian countries or those of democracies abroad.

Emerging technologies will also change the ways that autocrats deliver propaganda. State- controlled online "bots" (automated accounts) already plague social media. During Russia's 2014 invasion of Crimea and in the months afterward, for example, researchers at New York University found that fully half of the tweets from accounts that focused on Russian politics were both- generated. The October 2018 murder of Washington Post columnist Jamal Khashoggi prompted a surge in messaging from pro-regime Saudi bots.

Facial recognition technology is demonstrated at the Tiandy Technology Co. headquarters in Tianjin, China, last month. But bots will soon be indistinguishable from humans online capable of denouncing anti-regime activists, attacking rivals and amplifying state messaging in alarmingly lifelike ways. Lisa-Marie Neudert, a researcher with Oxford's Computational Propaganda Project, has warned that "the next generation of bots is preparing for attack. This time around, political bots will leave repetitive, automated tasks behind and instead become intelligent." The kind of tech advances that fuel Amazon's Alexa and Apple's Siri, she told the International Forum for Democratic Studies last October, are also teaching propaganda bots how to talk.

For years, the Chinese government has employed what is known as the "50 Cent Army"—thousands of fakes, paid commenters—to post online messages favorable to Beijing and to distract online critics. In the future, bots will do the work of the current legions of regime-paid desk workers.

These increasingly insidious bots will work together with other new tools to let dictatorships spread disinformation, including "deep fakes"— digital forgeries impossible to distinguish from authentic audio, video or images. Audio fakeries are already getting good enough to fool many listeners: Speech-synthesis systems made by companies such as Lyrebird (which says it creates "the most realistic artificial voices in the world") require as little as one minute of original voice recording to generate seemingly authentic audio of the target speaker. The video is soon to follow. On YouTube, one can already see an unnerving mashup of actors Steve Buscemi and Jennifer Lawrence and a far-from- perfect video made by the Chinese company iFlytek showing both Donald Trump and Barack Obama "speaking" in fluent Mandarin. Soon, such fakes will be chillingly convincing. That will leave those playing defense "outgunned," according to Dartmouth computer science professor Hany Farid. There are probably 100 to 1,000 times "more people developing the technology to manipulate content than there is to detect [it]," he told Pew in January. "Suddenly there will be the ability to claim that anything is fake. And how are we going to believe anything?"

> *"THE KIND OF ADVANCES IN AI THAT FUEL ALEXA AND SIRI ARE ALSO TEACHING PROPAGANDA 'BOTS' HOW TO TALK."*

New tools will also make it possible for dictators to conduct surveillance as never before, both online and in the real world. Humans are training computers to identify and interpret emotional context within blocks of text using natural language processing (an application of machine learning). Facebook now uses similar techniques to examine linguistic nuances in posts that might flag users who are contemplating suicide. Smaller companies are working to score individual social- media posts based on attitude, emotion and intent. The California-based AI startup Predictim scoured the text of Twitter, Facebook and Instagram to develop risk ratings for (of all things) wannabe babysitters. Based solely on the language in potential babysitters' social-media postings, the app provided automated assessments of their propensity to bully, be disrespectful or use drugs. The startup's efforts triggered a swift backlash last year, but China, Russia and other autocracies will not share such scruples. Jack Clark, who directs policy for the research firm OpenAI, warns that "we currently aren't—at a national or international level—assessing or measuring the rate of progress of AI capabilities and the ease with which given capabilities can be modified for malicious purposes." This, he adds, "is equivalent to flying blind into a tornado—eventually, something's going to hit you."

The next generation of natural language processing tools will become more sophisticated as advances in machine learning accelerate. Applied by the wrong regime, they can be combined with other data to assess an individual's trustworthiness, patriotism and likelihood of dissenting.

Such applications do not yet exist, but an early move in that direction can be seen in

China's public statements. As The Wall Street Journal has reported, "By 2020, the government hopes to implement a national 'social credit' system that would assign every citizen a rating based on how they behave at work, in public venues and in their financial dealings." Local governments across China are already keeping digital records of citizens' behavior and docking them for jaywalking, breaking family-planning rules or paying bills late. Those who end up on the blacklist lose out, unable to buy high-speed train tickets, obtain government subsidies, purchase real estate or even get hired. According to a plan issued by Beijing's municipal government, by 2021, the capital's blacklisted citizens will be "unable to move even a single step."

Venezuela has introduced its own "carnet de la patria" (fatherland card), a smart-chip-based piece of identification that citizens need to get access to government services such as health care and subsidized food. Human Rights Watch reports that the card may capture voting history as well. The data that this system generates is stored by the Chinese company ZTE, which has also reportedly deployed a team of experts within Venezuela's state-run telecommunications company CANTV to help run the program, according to a 2018 investigation by Reuters.

Yoshua Bengio, a computer scientist known as one of the three "godfathers" of deep learning in AI, recently described to Bloomberg his concerns about the growing use of technology for political control. "This is the 1984 Big Brother Scenario," he said, "I think it's becoming more and more scary." Autocrats' ability to spy on their citizens will be further enhanced by advances in artificial intelligence that make sense of enormous data sets. In both the U.S. and China, companies are optimizing new chips to support neural networks and algorithmic approach loosely inspired by human brain function.

China's Ministry of Industry and Information Technology recently said that it hoped to mass-produce neural-network optimized chips by 2020. They will allow oppressive regimes to collect information more efficiently on their population's speech and behavior, sift through massive data sets and quickly exploit the information.

One particular application of AI—facial recognition—could be as ubiquitous in a decade as smartphone cameras are today. The technology has been used by the U.S. Department of Homeland Security, San Diego's Police Department, and others to enhance security at large events like the Super Bowl. In the hands of autocrats, however, technology has great potential for repressive use. Chinese police deployed facial-recognition glasses in early 2018, and Beijing-based LLVision Technology Co. sells basic versions to countries in Africa and Europe. Such glasses can be used to help identify criminals like thieves and drug dealers—or to hunt human- rights activists and pro-democracy protesters.

A political dissident in Harare may soon have as much to fear as a heroin smuggler in Zhengzhou: The Chinese AI firm CloudWalk Technology has sold Zimbabwe's government a mass facial- recognition system. It will send facial data on millions of Zimbabweans back to the company in China, allowing it to refine its algorithms and perfect the system for further export. Business is also booming for other companies. The global client list of the Chinese surveillance firm Tiandy, a CCTV camera manufacturer and "smart security solution provider," includes more than sixty countries.

The rise of new "smart cities" around the world could also mean trouble. Autocratic regimes will be able to weave diverse data streams into a grid of social control. China plans to build more smart cities like Yinchuan, where commuters can use a positive facial ID to board a bus, or Hangzhou, where facial data can be used to buy a meal at KFC. Planned megacities like Xiong'an New Area, a development southwest of Beijing, suggest the shape of future panopticons. These cities of the future could use centralized systems of control across financial, criminal and government records, drawing on websites, visual imagery, phone applications and sensors—all of it propelled by 5G data transmission.

Until quite recently, it was easy to see the digital revolution as a great liberalizer, a way to transmit ideas faster than any would-be censor could react. The reality is turning out to be far more complicated.

The internet dispersed data, but new technological advances can concentrate its power in the hands of a few. With more than thirty billion devices expected to be connected to the internet by 2020, each one generating new data, those who can control, process, and exploit the information rush will have a major advantage. A regime bent on stability may feel virtually compelled to do so.

But we should not assume that the benefits will accrue only to repressive governments. When dictatorships sought in recent years to monitor their citizens' online communications, the U.S. State Department and others sponsored encryption tools that allowed would-be dissenters to safely communicate. When regimes censored information and blocked access to key websites, circumvention tools cropped up to allow unfettered access.

That is the right idea. Open societies will need to marshal an array of responses in the contest ahead. Democracies will need to slap sanctions on the individuals and groups using new tools for repressive ends, inflict higher costs on technology companies complicit in gross human-rights abuses, invest in countermeasures and harden their own systems against external intrusions.

Free governments will also have to differentiate between using new technologies for legitimate purposes (such as traditional law enforcement) and using them to solidify single-party control, curtail basic rights and meddle in democracies abroad.

Dictators from Caracas to Pyongyang will seek to exploit the enormous potential for political misuse inherent in emerging technologies, just as they have over the decades with radio, television, and the internet itself. Democracies will need to be ready to fight back.

Mr. Fontaine is the CEO of the Center for a New American Security in Washington, D.C. Ms. Frederick is an associate fellow in the center's technology and security program and worked previously for Facebook, the U.S. Naval Special Warfare Command, and the Department of Defense.[xlii]

Figure 20 Hip Hop and Streaming | Patriot Act with Hasan Minhaj | Netflix

manualforgorillas.com

"The concept of the benevolent dictator, just like the concepts of the noble thief or the honest whore, is no more than a meaningless fantasy."
Alaa Al Aswany

The new Gorillas: Venezuela's Armed Forces

As Venezuelan and former Army Officer, IS A SHAME witness how my fellow Army mates of the Gran Mariscal de Ayacucho, Class of 1993, following the steps to others Classes from 1971, 1985, 1987 and 1990, actively participated, since the beginning of the so-called Bolivarian Revolution in 1998 and still today keep working on stealing and/or giving away the Resources of the Country, needed by millions of families, included mine and theirs in most of the cases[xliii], to foreign Countries and Corporations. I spent more time with most of you than with my own brother Gustavo Adolfo, you my fellow friends and brothers, including many of other classes that I met and worked with, shared work experiences, at the Military Academy of Venezuela, in Service as Officer or Public Servant, you that supported and still support the Nicolas Maduro's Regime, BECAME INTO THE NEW GORILLAS OF THE CENTURY XXI, sponsored by Russia, China, Iran, Syria and a bunch of other Dictatorial Regimes I already mentioned in the Chapters before this.

Venezuela 2017 Human Rights Report

This is the executive summary of this report[xliv]: Venezuela is formally a multiparty, constitutional republic, but for more than a decade, political power has been concentrated in a single party with an increasingly authoritarian executive exercising significant control over the legislative, judicial, citizens,' and electoral branches of government. The Supreme Court determined Nicolas Maduro to have won the 2013 presidential elections amid allegations of pre- and post-election fraud, including government interference, the use of state resources by the ruling party, and voter manipulation. The opposition gained super majority two-thirds control of the National Assembly in the 2015 legislative elections. The executive branch, however, used its control over the Supreme Court (TSJ) to weaken the National Assembly's constitutional role to legislate, ignore the separation of powers, and enable the president to govern through a series of emergency decrees.

Civilian authorities maintained effective, although politicized, control over the security forces.

Democratic governance and human rights deteriorated dramatically during the year as the result of a campaign of the Maduro administration to consolidate its power.

On March 30, the TSJ annulled the National Assembly's constitutional functions, threatened to abolish parliamentary immunity, and assumed significant control over social, economic, legal, civil, and military policies. The TSJ's actions triggered large-scale street protests through the spring and summer in which approximately 125 persons died. Security forces and armed pro- government paramilitary groups known as "colectivos" at times used excessive force against protesters.

Credible nongovernmental organizations (NGOs) reported indiscriminate household raids, arbitrary arrests, and the use of torture to deter protesters. The government arrested thousands of individuals, tried hundreds of civilians in military tribunals, and sentenced approximately twelve opposition mayors to 15-month prison terms for alleged failure to control protests in their areas.

On May 1, President Maduro announced plans to rewrite the 1999 constitution, and on July 30, the government held fraudulent elections, boycotted by the opposition, to select representatives for a National Constituent Assembly (ANC). On August 4, the ANC adopted a "coexistence decree" that effectively neutralized other branches of government. Throughout the year the government arbitrarily stripped the civil rights of opposition leaders to not allow them to run for public office. On October 15, the government held gubernatorial elections overdue since December 2016.

The ruling United Socialist Party (PSUV) maintained it won 17 of the 23 governors' seats, although the election was fraught with deficiencies, including a lack of independent, credible international observers, last-minute changes to polling station locations with limited public notice, manipulation of ballot layouts, limited voting locations in opposition neighborhoods, and a lack of technical audit for the National Electoral Council's (CNE) tabulation. The regime then called for mayoral elections on December 10, with numerous irregularities favoring government candidates.

The most significant human rights issues included extrajudicial killings by security forces, including government sponsored "colectivos;" torture by security forces; harsh and life-threatening prison conditions; widespread arbitrary detentions; and political prisoners. The government unlawfully interfered with privacy rights, used military courts to try civilians, and ignored judicial orders to release prisoners. The government routinely blocked signals, interfered with the operations, or shut down privately owned television, radio, and other media outlets. The law criminalized criticism of the government, and the government threatened violence and detained journalists critical of the government, used violence to repress peaceful demonstrations, and placed legal restrictions on the ability of NGOs to receive foreign funding. Other issues included interference with freedom of movement; establishment of illegitimate institutions to replace democratically elected representatives; pervasive corruption and impunity among all security forces and in other national and state government offices, including at the highest levels; violence against women, including lethal violence; trafficking in persons; and the worst forms of child labor, which the government made minimal efforts to eliminate.

The government took no effective action to combat impunity that pervaded all levels of the civilian bureaucracy and the security forces.

Amnesty International Report 2017/18: Venezuela

Venezuela remained in a state of emergency, repeatedly extended since January 2016. A National Constituent Assembly was elected without the participation of the opposition. The Attorney General was dismissed under irregular circumstances. Security forces continued to use excessive and undue force to disperse protests. Hundreds of people were arbitrarily detained. There were many reports of torture and other ill- treatment, including sexual violence against demonstrators. The judicial system continued to be used to silence dissidents, including using military authority to prosecute civilians. Human rights defenders were harassed, intimidated and subject to raids. Conditions of detention were extremely harsh. The food and health crises continued to worsen, especially affecting children, people with chronic illness and pregnant women. The number of Venezuelans seeking asylum in other countries increased[xlv].

Human Rights Watch Country Summary: Venezuela

In Venezuela today, no independent government institutions remain to act as a check on executive power. The Venezuelan government—under Maduro and previously under Chávez—has stacked the courts with judges who make no pretense of independence. The government has been repressing dissent through often-violent crackdowns on street protests, jailing opponents, and prosecuting civilians in military courts. It has also stripped power from the opposition-led legislature. Due to severe shortages of medicines, medical supplies, and food, many Venezuelans cannot adequately feed their families or access the most basic healthcare. In response to the human rights and humanitarian crisis, hundreds of thousands of Venezuelans are fleeing the country. Other persistent concerns include poor prison conditions, impunity for human rights violations, and harassment by government officials of human rights defenders and independent media outlets. Persecution of Political Opponents the Venezuelan government has jailed political opponents and disqualified them from running for office. At time of writing, more than 340 political prisoners were languishing in Venezuelan prisons or intelligence services headquarters, according to the Penal Forum, a Venezuelan network of pro-bono criminal defense lawyers. In mid-2017, the Supreme Court sentenced five opposition mayors, after summary proceedings that violated international norms of due process to 15 months in prison and disqualified them from running for office. At time of writing, one was being held at the intelligence services' headquarters in Caracas; the rest had fled the country. At least nine or two more mayors were subject to a Supreme Court injunction that could lead to similarly long prison sentences if they are accused of violating it. Opposition leader Leopoldo López is serving a 13-year sentence for allegedly inciting violence during a demonstration in Caracas in February 2014, despite the lack of any credible evidence against him. After three-and-a-half years in prison, López was moved to house arrest in July 2017, but was again detained in the middle of the night weeks later after he publicly criticized the government. That same night, intelligence agents detained Antonio Ledezma, a former opposition mayor who has been under house arrest since 2015 and published a critical video while under house arrest. The Supreme Court later issued a statement saying López was forbidden from carrying out "political proselytism" and that Ledezma could not "issue statements to any media," adding that "intelligence sources" said they had a plan to flee. Both men were returned to house arrest days later. In November, Ledezma fled Venezuela. Several others arrested in connection with the 2014 anti-government protests or subsequent political activism remain under house arrest or in detention awaiting trial. Crackdown on Protest Activity Venezuelan security forces, together with armed pro-government groups called "colectivos," have violently attacked anti- government protests—some of them attended by tens of thousands of Venezuelans—between April and July 2017. Security force personnel have shot demonstrators at point-blank range with riot-control munitions, run over demonstrators with an armored vehicle, brutally beaten people who offered no resistance, and staged violent raids on apartment buildings. The Attorney General's Office reported that, as of July 31, 124 people had been killed during incidents related to the protests. The UN High Commissioner for Human Rights reported in August that more than half of the deaths had been caused by security agents or colectivos. The Venezuelan government claims that ten security force officers died in the context of the three demonstrations and reported several instances of violence against government supporters. In late July, before the Constituent Assembly fired Attorney General Luisa Ortega Díaz, her office was investigating nearly 2,000 cases of people injured during the crackdown. While the number appears to have included cases in which protesters and security forces were the alleged perpetrators, in more than half of the cases the office had evidence suggesting fundamental rights violations. About 5,400 people were arrested in connection with demonstrations between April and November, including demonstrators, bystanders, and people taken away from their homes without warrants, according to the Penal Forum. Around 3,900 had been conditionally released at time of writing but remained subject to criminal prosecution. Security forces have committed serious abuses against detainees that in some cases amount to torture— including severe beatings, the use of electric shocks, asphyxiation, and sexual abuse. Military courts have prosecuted more than 750 civilians in violation of international law. In early 2014, the government had also responded to massive anti- government protests with excessive force. Security forces often held protestors incommunicado on military bases for 48 hours or more, and in some cases, committed egregious human rights violations, including severe beatings, electric shocks, or burns, and forcing detainees to squat or kneel without moving for hours. No senior officers have been prosecuted for these abuses[xlvi].

Get rid of the other Gorillas.

The enigma of military assassinations in Venezuela

The mystery covers the growing wave of murders of retired and active officers in the country, almost always members of the Army and the National Guard. In recent months it has become a recurring theme. And the strangest thing is that the military institution does not seem to be sensitized to such atrocious acts that rarely have an answer. We could blame everyday criminal violence, but something else seems to be happening in the cases of these murdered soldiers. Let us see some of the most talked about cases in 2016 and so far in 2017.

2016

January 2016: The second GNB sergeants, Jean Carlos Méndez Alfonzo (22) and Luis Manuel Delgado Cao (20) shot dead in the Mendoza sector of the national highway, Troncal 9 de Barlovento. They guarded fifteen buses with PDVSA workers who were going to sign the collective contract. Mendez's father assures that they went without weapons and without bulletproof vests. In Trunk 9 they were intercepted by armed men who forced them to leave the vehicle. They killed the officers whose corpses were found in a forested area of Caucagua.

March 10, 2016: Four criminals murdered Lieutenant Colonel José Francisco Cedeño D Marco (45), in the sector The Council of La Victoria, Aragua state.

March 25, 2016: A National Guard official was riding a motorcycle when several criminals attacked him with long weapons. He died in the place. That happened at the entrance of Cota 905, Caracas.

April 15, 2016: In the early morning they killed two soldiers in different areas of Caracas. The GNB Captain Luis Alberto Chacón Hernández, assigned to the Redi Sur of El Paraíso, killed by several shots, when being with his wife and a friend, was intercepted by four criminals in Los Caobos.

April 15, 2016: Army Lieutenant, José Ramón Mendoza assassinated in the Kennedy District of Las Adjuntas, when he was traveling by motorcycle. They presume to steal your belongings.

April 17, 2016: GNB captain José Hernández Araujo (40) and his wife María Hernández Caruso (30) murdered in Guárico.

May 17, 2016: The sergeant of the Militia, Jesús Eduardo Guaramato Vásquez (34) shot dead in the head, in a restaurant at kilometer nine of the Petare-Santa Lucía highway, Sucre municipality, Miranda.

May 18, 2016: Felix Velásquez, retired Major General was killed in Santa Monica, Caracas. For the fact they captured two assassins.

May 29, 2016: The Army's first sergeant Juan Manuel Pérez (35) was killed when he was shot inside his truck at the Monte Piedad sector on January 23, Caracas. The regulation weapon was stolen. It was assigned to the guard of the facilities of the Stock Exchange of the BCV.

July 12, 2016: The first sergeant of the National Guard, José Edicto Alejos Sevilla, was in commission of services in the Foundation of the Movement for Peace and Life based in Miraflores, shot dead when he arrived at his residence in urban planning City Tiuna, by Car.

August 27, 2016: The lieutenant of the Venezuelan Air Force, Deini Paola Marín Gómez

(21) was killed by three shots in the face; and his father, Néstor José Marín Rodríguez, was given five in the thorax. It was in La Victoria, Aragua.

September 10, 2016: The second corporal of the Junior Army of Jesús Marquina Escalona (24), detached in Fuerte Tiuna, was killed when unidentified individuals intercepted him and shot him. It was in the sector La Peña, municipality Carache, on the road from Trujillo to Lara was with his son and his godson, in the avenue Las Turas of sector I of the urbanization Patarata, in Barquisimeto, Lara. Two men approached by motorcycle and one of them pointed a revolver at him; he asked for the cell phone, but the soldier ran, and the criminal shot him.

December 22, 2016: Assassinated the retired general of the National Guard, Alberto Silva Bohórquez (70). It was the military prosecutor who condemned the participants of the attempted coup against Carlos Andrés Pérez. His body was located in an advanced state of decomposition, inside the apartment he had rented recently in the Coribaita building on Los Apamates Street between Florida and Sabana Grande in Caracas. It would have been a robbery, according to the police. He was killed after hitting him with a bat.

December 24, 2016: The first sergeant Wilmer Enrique Vielma Montilla (29 years) died when a group of criminals attacked eight officers of the People's Guard, in the sector April 19, Pozo Verde parish, via El Pao, Bolivar state, when they escorted food trucks. Wounded were the second sergeants Muñoz Izarra and Peñalver Robles.

2017

January 9, 2017: GNB sergeant José Luis Miquilena (25), was shot dead in the head; It happened a few meters from the General Command of that military component in the El Paraíso parish.

January 24, 2017: The second sergeant major of the Army, Henry Rafael Salazar Carvette (47) was murdered, in the early hours of the morning, when armed subjects shot him in the head, which caused him death instantly. That was in street one, housing Nr. 3, urbanization Los Mangos de Santa Cruz, municipality Lamas de Aragua. Salazar left his house for his job in the Legal Department of Fuerte Tiuna when he was subjected and forced to return to his house where he was murdered.

February 5, 2017: First Lieutenant Alexis Jesús Pacheco Cárdenas (30) was killed, with a firearm, in Cagua, Aragua state, for alleged revenge. Several men intercepted him and, without saying a word, shot him. They presume revenge as a motive.

19 February 2017: The first sergeant Jesses Enrique Alburua Linares (46) belonging to group 10 of the Military Aviation and head of

the Department of Spare Parts of the Valencia Metro, was killed in Villa de Cura, Aragua. He was getting ready to buy hot dogs, at a fast-food stand, when two motorcycle riders came to assault. They shot the officer, who died shortly afterwards. The military was part of the group that attempted a coup against Carlos Andrés Pérez in 1992.

February 28, 2017: The second GNB sergeant, Darwin Renzo Manzano Romero (22), was shot in the neck when criminals attacked the GNB control point in the Delirio sector, Andrés Bello municipality, Miranda. José García (37) and Anthony Sanz were injured.

March 01, 2017: The sergeant of the GNB, Nixon José Donquiz Jayaliyu (28), was shot dead in the occipital, in the railroad terminal of Cúa, Miranda. "It is presumed that he was killed to steal the gun," according to the official version.

March 03, 2017: Officer Jesús Caraballo Briceño assassinated when he supplied his motorcycle with gasoline in the Avenida Fuerzas Armadas de Caracas.

March 4, 2017: Frigate Lieutenant Víctor Hugo Cabrera Molina (39), killed when he was traveling through El Rosal, Caracas. He lost control of the vehicle and crashed into the road's defenses after being shot in the chest. "Possibly to try to assault him".

09 March 2017: A commission of GNB officials was mobilized to the Villa Belén sector, entrance to the bunker, via El Pao, Caroní municipality, Bolívar. There they faced a group of criminals who murdered the second sergeant Luis Armando Contreras.

March 12, 2017: The eldest of the Bolivarian National Guard, Emigdio José Medina Rondón (40) was killed in the early morning hours. It is presumed that he was persecuted by some individuals to steal his vehicle when he was going to his home in the El Ingenio de Guatire sector, Miranda state.[xlvii]

Military prisoners

The Venezuelan military prisons are overcrowded by the large number of officers and troop personnel who are being prosecuted or investigated on suspicion or indications of not supporting the Government of Nicolás Maduro; 152 are conspiracy marks and charged for crimes such as Treason of the Fatherland, Instigation to the Rebellion or Against the Military Decor. In this list we do not include those who remain with a house by jail or with precautionary presentation measures. Nor are the hundreds of soldiers detained for common crimes.

But let's see who these 152 military prisoners are for not agreeing with the current

Venezuelan political model, and that the retired General of Aviation, Eduardo Caldera, refreshes in this report because as he himself indicates "this list is very dynamic and subject to changes for multiple reasons, but the main objective is to inform the national and international community that in our country there are military political prisoners. "

The main military prison in Venezuela is the Military Processing Center of Ramo Verde, located in the Miranda state a few kilometers from Caracas. At this moment they have almost a month without water; the toilets are rotten, and the prison director says they cannot buy water by cistern because they do not have money. Family members must bring prepared food.

Army Component

There are seventy-one prisoners of this force: a General in Chief, a Major General, 8 Colonels, ten lieutenant colonels, two majors, three captains, fourteen first lieutenants, eight lieutenants, 24 sergeants and a second corporal. One of the largest components of the Bolivarian National Armed Forces (FANB), there is a general in chief, Raúl Isaías Baduel, who is the highest level of the armed institution. He was arrested on 03/04/2009 and then arrested again from January 12, 2017, and transferred to the Tomb of the Bolivarian Intelligence Service

(SEBIN), as it is known to the cells housed in the central building of the agency.

There is also the Major General (EJ) Miguel Rodríguez Torres, arrested on March 13, 2018; participated in the coup attempt led by Hugo Chávez on February 4, 1992, during the Government of Chavez was head of SEBIN and with Nicolás Maduro was the Minister of Interior and Justice.

7 Army Colonels arrested: José Gregorio Delgado Vásquez (prison of La Pica, Maturín), Rafael Antonio Bendaham Couthino, Ricardo Zomacal Luongo (arrested on 03/03/17), Ramón Velasco García (arrested on 09/20/18 by the case of the drones on 04/08/18 in the parade of the National Guard), José Manuel Carrillo Venera, Waldemar Briceño García, Jonni Mejías Laya (arrested on 01/31/19).

10 Lieutenants Colonels: Ovidio Carrasco (Chief of Communications of the Honor Guard of the Presidency of the Republic, arrested on 02/11/19), Carlos Urbina Velásquez (Operation Armagedón), Henry José Medina Gutiérrez (detained on 03/02/1999) 18), Durvis Enrique Meleán Vargas, Deivis Mota Marrero (detained since 02/03/18), Victor Eduardo Soto Méndez, Igbert José Marín Chaparro, Juan Carlos Peña Palmentieri, Freddy Mogollón, Juan Carlos Ramos.

2 Majors: Nehomar Castro Hidalgo, Carlos Alfonso Parra Pérez.

3 Captains: Anyelo Julio Heredia Gervacio, Pulido Gómez (arrested since 10/05/18), Jorge Enrique Pérez Castañeda.

14 First Lieutenants: Iván Jesús Marín Martínez (arrested on 02/17/19 for allegedly attempting to create a sniper unit of the 25th Army Brigade), Luis Alejandro Mogollón Velásquez (arrested on 04/08/17, administratively demoted on 28 / 04/18, requires medical attention for seizures and kidney problems), Eliecer Vásquez Guillén (administratively degraded on 03/02/18), Alexander Infante Silva, José Alejandro Moreno, Gabriel Jefferson García Dos Ramos (administratively degraded), Simón Torres Varela, Eduardo Pérez Amaya, Vladimir Ilich Aguilera (arrested on 10/01/2017), Alberto Alejandro Maita Espinoza, Gustavo Sandoval Quintero, Yeiber Ariza Apolinar, Oswaldo José Gutiérrez Guevara (detained since 06/08/17, Fort Paramacay case), Méndez Chacón.

8 Lieutenants: Rafael Jackson Hernandez, Luciano Enrique Torres Borges, Franklin Duran Parra, Jose Gabriel Parra Castillo, Luis Alberto Hernandez Medina, Asel Chinevel Hernandez, Angel Bernal, Cintia Lopez.

2 Major Sergeants: Noel Ricardo Romero Lugo, Jairo Eli Villegas Moreno.

4 Sergeants Seconds: Darwin Antonio Solís Benítez, Giulianny Espinoza Ramírez,

Willy Daniel Solórzano Méndez, Andy Hinar Martínez Figueroa.

17 First Sergeants: Yecson Enrique Lozada, Rubén Augusto Bermúdez Oviedo, Juan Francisco Díaz Castillo, Yoelvis José Villalobos Fernández, Javier Rafael Peña, Víctor Alejandro Sosa González, Feydi Rafael Montero, Cristian Estrada (Fort Paramacay case), Neomar Brito Malavé (Paramacay case), Cesar Balzán Balzán, Jesús Bermúdez Villegas, Nervis Rincón Redondo, Luis Manuel Tezara Flores, Williams José Saragay Arias, Kenny Jiménez Rodríguez, Jesús Tarazona, Franyer Argenis Meléndez,

Sergeant Supervisor Julio Cesar Gutiérrez.

Second Private Alberto Polo Díaz, imputed for rebellion, detained on 06/08/2017.

Navy

There are a total of 22 Navy officials, most of whom were arrested in 2018 for the denunciation of a captain and an admiral. There are 2 Navy captains detained, one Corvette Captain, 8 Navy Lieutenants, 11 Frigate Lieutenant and a Second Sergeant. They are:

2 Navy Captains: Luis Humberto De La Sotta Quiroga, Javier José Díaz Ugas.

Corvette Captain Gustavo Macsotay Rauseo, imputed for instigation to the rebellion on 05/23/18.

8 Navy Lieutenants: Daniel Alejandro Labrador Lugo, Antonio Julio Scola Lugo,

Gustavo Carrero Angarita, Anderson José Fernández Aguilar, Roberto Molina, José Luis Rodríguez Gómez, José Efraín Pinto Calderón, José Luis Noriega Manrique.

10 Frigate Lieutenants: Gregorio Ramón Zárraga, Jackson Eduardo Brown Uzcátegui, Lino José Pire Ramos, Erwin Tulio Rivero Balza, Paul Enrique Machado Briceño, Noel Francisco Berroterán Camacho, Noel Adrián Arturo Díaz Dente, Alonzo José Rodríguez Petit, Pedro José Jiménez Maestre, Jean Franco García.

Second sergeant Jesus David Amaya Oliveras, imputed for instigation to the rebellion on 02/09/18, arrest in CENAPROMIL Ramo Verde.

Military Aviation

This component of the Bolivarian National Armed Forces is in prison for crimes related to the conspiracy: a Major General, a Colonel, 2 Lieutenant Colonels, 4 Majors, 3 Captains, a First Lieutenant, and a Lieutenant. They are:

General of Division Oswaldo Hernández, sentenced to almost 9 years, has cancer in the neck, treatment of chemotherapy, radiotherapy, and surgery. Blue Strike Case.

Colonel Juan Pablo Saavedra Mejías, imputed for instigation to the rebellion on 05/23/18.

2 Lieutenants Colonels: Ruperto Chiquinquirá, Sánchez Casares (case of Golpe

Azul), Ruperto Molina Ramírez, imputed for instigation to the rebellion.

4 Majors: Leonardo De Gouveia, Víctor José Ascanio, César Orta Santamaría and Ricardo Efraín González Torres.

3 Captains: Nery Córdova, Moreno, Andrés Thompson Martínez, Jesús Enrique Salazar Moncada (sentenced to 10 years and then sentenced for admission of the facts in a new trial to almost 5 years).

First Lieutenant Luis Lugo, arrested on 02/11/15, left for benefit on 10/11/18, arrested again on 10/14/18, serving his sentence of almost five years.

Lieutenant Peter Moreno, arrested on 02/12/15, left for benefit on 10/11/18, detained again that same day, serving his sentence for almost 5 years.

Bolivarian National Guard

It is the most active general component in prison, five in total, in addition to 3 Colonels, a Lieutenant Colonel, two Majors, 4 Captains, 2 Lieutenants, a sergeant major, 3 sergeants major third, 7 sergeants first and 18 sergeants second.

2 Division Generals: Pedro Naranjo Suárez, Alejandro Pérez Gámez (case of drones).

3 Brigade Generals: Nelson Morantes Guitian, Héctor Hernández Da Costa, Edward Castellanos Jáuregui (case of the drones).

3 Colonels: Juan Francisco Rodríguez Dos Ramos (he was assigned to the Ministry of Defense when he was arrested at the end of March 2019), Pedro Javier Zambrano Hernández (arrested on 08/12/18, case of the drones), Oswaldo García Palomo.

Lieutenant Colonel José de Jesús Gámez Bustamante, arrested on 01/21/15, charged with terrorism and association to commit a crime, convicted, is in critical conditions of malnutrition.

2 Majors: Abraham Américo Suarez Ramos (arrested for instigation of the rebellion on 05/28/18, was tortured, tried to commit suicide and without being recovered was removed from the hospital without medical order and again detained in the DGCIM), retired Major Raúl Roberto Castillo Gallardo (arrested on 12/15/18).

4 Captains: Juan Carlos Nieto Quintero (date of arrest 22/04/2009, Golpe Azul), Carlos Luis Jiménez Alfonzo (arrested on 11/23/15), Jesús María Alarcón Camacho, Juan Carlos Caguaripano Scott (arrested on 30/07 / 2017, administratively degraded on 03/02/18, was the leader of the Fort Paramacay case).

2 Lieutenants: Paul Machado (sentenced to almost 5 years in prison for publicly breaking the card of the fatherland and also instigating rebellion and lack of military decorum), Pedro Márquez (charged with instigation of the

rebellion since 28/05 / 18). Sergeant Major Gabriel Jesus Barros Romero, imputed for instigation to the rebellion.

3 Sergeants Major of Third: Luis Alexander Bandres Figueroa (detained on 01/22/19 for military rebellion in National Guard unit in Cotiza, Caracas), with him also Martínez Natera, Castro Álvarez.

7 First Sergeants: for the case of rebellion in Cotiza: Piñango Salas, Rico Arrieta, Milanes Chirinos, Camacaro Gonzalez, Rivero Gonzalez, Yoander Jose Blanco Rondon, Erick Javier Gonzalez Azuaje.

18 Sergeants Seconds: some for the rebellion case in Cotiza: González Carrasco, Romero Aguinagalde, Romero Pérez, Pérez Soler, Hernández Palma, Montero Mujica, Lobo Medina, Piña Oviedo, Luis Chirinos, Salcedo Méndez, Glok Vásquez Charly Ramírez, Peña Arteaga, Díaz Vivenes, Carrillo Santana, González Hospedales, Gregory Ojeda Alonso, Javier Rafael Peña Quintana, Jesus Eduardo Araque (detained on 02/21/17, Second Military Court of Accidental Maracay Trial, imputed for instigating the rebellion, outrage to the sentinel).

This total of 46 soldiers of the National Guard, 13 of the Military Aviation, 22 of the Navy and 71 of the Army, are the best demonstration of what is happening in Venezuela with the military institution. Never before in the Venezuelan democratic history were so many soldiers detained for political reasons, many of them subjected to brutal physical and psychological torture, as well as brutal mistreatment and threats to their families.

There are two prisons with military annexes: that of La Pica in Maturín and that of the Penitentiary Center of the West (CPO) Cárcel de Santa Ana. There are also detainees in the General Directorate of Military Counterintelligence (DGCIM), the Bolivarian Intelligence Service (SEBIN) and Military Police of Fort Tiuna.[xlviii]

GET THE REFERENCES

I really want to thank you for your purchase of this book, I'm in exile and left behind my Parents, Sisters, Family, Friends and Neighbors and I cannot rest trying to pay my bills in US and send them food and money to survive the Humanitarian Crisis they are experiencing. Part of the money you paid for this book was already sent to them, also if you get some of these references I may get commission from the sale.

I hardly recommend you watch the Movie "Fer-pect" Crime, you will laugh a lot, guaranteed!

Regards!

CC: English Audio: Spanish

manualforgorillas.com

The Author

Juan Ramon Rodulfo Moya, **Defined by Nature**: Inhabitant of Planet Earth, Human, Son of Eladio Rodulfo and Briceida Moya, Brother of Gabriela, Gustavo and Katiuska, Father of Gabriel and Sofia; **Defined by society**: Venezuelan Citizen (Limited Human Rights by default), Friend of many, enemy of few, Neighbor, Student/Teacher/Student, Worker/Supervisor/Manager/Leader/Worker, Husband of K/Ex-Husband of K/Husband of Y; **Defined by the U.S. Immigration Office**: Legal Alien; **Classroom studies**: Master's Degree in Human Resource Management, English, Mandarin Chinese; **Real-World Studies**: Human Behavior; **Home Studios**: SEO Webmaster, Graphic Design, Application and Website Development, Internet and Social Media Marketing, Video Production, YouTube Branding, Part 107 Commercial Drone Pilot, Import-Export, Affiliate Marketing, Cooking, Laundry, Home Cleaning; **Work experience**: Public-Private-Entrepreneurial Sectors; **Other definitions:** Bitcoin Evangelist, Defender of Human Rights, Peace and Love.

Publications:

Books:

- Why Maslow: How to use his theory to stay in Power Forever (EN/SP)
- Asylum Seekers (EN/SP)
- Manual for Gorillas: 9 Rules to be the "Fer-pect" Dictator (EN/SP)
- Why you must Play the Lottery (EN/SP); Para Español Oprima #2: Speaking Spanish in Times of Xenophobia (EN/SP)
- Cause of Death: IGNORANCE | Human Behavior in Times of PANIC (EN/SP)
- Politics explained for Millennials, GENs XYZ and future generations (EN/SP)
- Las cenizas del Ejército Libertador (EN/SP)
- Remain Silent: The only right we have. The legal Aliens (EN/SP)
- Fortune Cookie Coaching 88 Motivational Tips Made of Fortune Cookies, Vol I (EN)
- Vicky Erotic Tales, Vol I (EN)

Blogs:

Noticias de Nueva Esparta, Ubuntu Café, Coffee Secrets, Guaripete Pro, Rodulfox, Red Wasp Drone, Barista Pro, Gorila Travel, Fortune Cookie Coach, All Books, Vicky Toys.

Audiovisual Productions:

Podcasts:
Ubuntu Cafe | Vicky Erotic Tales | Fortune Cookie Coach | All Books, available at: juanrodulfo.com/podcasts

Music:
Albums: Margarita | Race to Extinction | Relaxed Panda | Amazonia | Cassiopeia | Caracas | Arcoiris Musical | Close Your Eyes, disponibles en: juanrodulfo.com/music

Photography & Video:
On sale at Adobe Stock, iStock, Shutterstock, and Veectezy, available at: juanrodulfo.com/gallery

Social Media Profiles:

Twitter / FB / Instagram / TikTok/ VK / LinkedIn / Sina Weibo: @rodulfox

Google Author: https://g.co/kgs/grjtN5
Google Artist: https://g.co/kgs/H7Fiqg
Twitter: https://twitter.com/rodulfox
Facebook: https://facebook.com/rodulfox
LinkedIn: https://www.linkedin.com/in/rodulfox
Instagram: https://www.instagram.com/rodulfox/
VK: https://vk.com/rodulfox
TikTok: https://www.tiktok.com/@rodulfox

Trading View: https://www.tradingview.com/u/rodulfox/

Table of Contents

PREFACE 7
    Charlie Chaplin – Final speech from The Great Dictator..11
APOLOGIZE TO THE GORILLAS................. 15
WHAT IS A GORILLA MILITARY 19
    Origin of the expression in Argentina 19
        Later use in Latin America............... 21
RULE 1: Find The "Fer-pect" Place. 29
RULE 2: Get yourself a military uniform. 41
RULE 3: Learn to yell like a pregnant woman giving birth. 53
RULE 4: Do not waste time studying or even reading a book. 63
    Ho Chi Minh - Baker 63

    Pol Pot - Teacher 64

    Adolf Hitler - Artist 65

    Benito Mussolini - Author 65

    Than Shwe - Mailman 66

    Muammar Qaddafi - Goat Herder ...66

    Stalin - Weatherman 67

    Fidel Castro - Angry Ballplayer........67

    Nicolas Maduro - Bus Driver 68

    Kim Jong Un - Dictator Son.............68

    Saddam Hussein - Assassin 69

Anastasio Somoza García - Speak English/Spanish 69

Mao Zedong - Assistant librarian 70

Enver Hoxha - Tobacconist.............. 70

Nicolae Ceausescu - Shoemaker 71

Idi Amin - Doughnut Vendor........... 71

Josip Broz - Test driver for Daimler 72

Rafael Trujillo - Telegraph operator 73

Bashar al-Asad - Ophthalmologist... 73

François Duvalier - Doctor 74

RULE 5 Find the "Fer-pect" Enemy. 77
    Internal Scapegoats........................ 78

    External Enemies 79

    What Stalin Feared Most: Collusion Among Enemies 84

    "Enemy of the People" 86

RULE 6: Create or copy a Sticky Slogan, Jingle or Doctrine 91
    Dictatorship and Ideology................ 94

RULE 7: Have fun sending people to Jail, Killing or Disappearing the Opposition 101

RULE 8: Free Media? Jail'em All and create your own.. 109

RULE 9: Update your Business. 125
    China's 'techno-dystopia' 126

    Suppressing dissent 127

The new Gorillas: Venezuela's Armed Forces 143
Venezuela 2017 Human Rights Report 144
Amnesty International Report 2017/18: Venezuela 147
Human Rights Watch Country Summary: Venezuela 148
Get rid of the other Gorillas. 152
Military prisoners........................... 158
   Army Component 159
   Navy 162
   Military Aviation 163
   Bolivarian National Guard 164
GET THE REFERENCES............................ 168
The Author 173
   Publications:................................. 174
   Books: 174
   Blogs: 174
Audiovisual Productions: 175
   Podcasts: 175
   Music: 175
   Photography & Video: 175
Social Media Profiles: 175
Notes 181

Notes

[i] Constitution of the Bolivarian Republic of Venezuela, Article 5. The sovereignty resides in the people, who exercise it directly in the manner provided in this Constitution and in the law, and indirectly, by suffrage, by the organisms that exercise the Public Power. The organs of the State emanate from popular sovereignty and to it they are subject.

[ii] Tarabay Jamie, CNN, Myanmar's military: The power Aung San Suu Kyi cannot control, updated 4:22 AM ET, Wed December 6, 2017, fetched from: https://www.cnn.com/2017/09/21/asia/myanmar-military-the-real-power/index.html

[iii] World Population Review, Dictatorship Countries 2019, fetched from: http://worldpopulationreview.com/countries/dictatorship-countries/

[iv] DPA/The Local, ever more people worldwide living under dictatorship, German study finds, 22 March 2018 10:15 CET+01:00, fetched from: https://www.thelocal.de/20180322/ever-more-people-worldwide-living-under-dictatorship-german-study-finds

[v] Other humans that eventually attended a Military Academy or went to real War.

[vi] Gorilla, From Wikipedia, the free encyclopedia, fetch from: https://en.wikipedia.org/wiki/Gorilla

[vii] Gorilla (politic denomination), Wikipedia the free encyclopedia, fetched from: https://es.wikipedia.org/wiki/Gorila_(denominación_política), Translated by: Juan Rodulfo

[viii] Johnny Angel, LA Weekly, Wednesday, September 26, 2001, fetched from: https://corpwatch.org/article/usa-its-oil-stupid

[ix] Jesus Crespo Cuaresma, Harald Oberhofer and Paul Raschky, Monash University, September 2010, fetched from: https://www.researchgate.net/publication/46448887_Oil_and_the_Duration_of_Dictatorships

[x] Lair Ribeiro, La Magia de la Comunicación, December 21, 1998, Editorial URANO

[xi] Morgan Meis, The Dictator's Speech, January 01st 2011, Retrieved April 12, 2019, from: https://thesmartset.com/article01311102/.

[xii] Reza Khany, Zohre Hamzelou, A Systemic Functional Analysis of Dictators' Speech: Toward a Move-based Model, International Conference on Current Trends in ELT, Procedia Social and Behavioral Sciences, 6 May 2014, Retrieved April 12, 2019, from: https://www.sciencedirect.com/science/article/pii/S1877042814025919

[xiii] WARNING: I am not against nor mocking the people that actually work and/or raised their families doing tasks as Bakers, Mailmen, Bus Drivers, and others mentioned ahead. I rather believe in the hearts of humans than in Certificates hanging in walls. Juan Rodulfo

[xiv] Blake Stilwell, The 9 day jobs of brutal dictators, Jan. 12, 2016, Retrieved April 12, 2019, from: https://www.wearethemighty.com/articles/the-9-day-jobs-of-brutal- dictators

[xv] 15 Before They Were Despots: Dictators and Their Old Jobs, February 2, 2007, Retrieved April 12, 2019, from: https://www.neatorama.com/2007/02/02/before-they-were-despots- dictators-and-their-old-jobs/

[xvi] THEFAMOUSPEOPLE, Kim Jong-un Biography, Retrieved April 12, 2019, from: https://www.thefamouspeople.com/profiles/kim-jong-un-5953.php

[xvii] THEFAMOUSPEOPLE, Saddam Hussein Biography, Retrieved April 12, 2019 from: https://www.thefamouspeople.com/profiles/saddam-hussein-95.php

[xviii] THEFAMOUSPEOPLE, Anastasio Somoza García Biography, Retrieved April 12, 2019 from: https://www.thefamouspeople.com/profiles/anastasio-somoza- garca-5875.php

[xix] THEFAMOUSPEOPLE, Mao Zedong Biography, Retrieved April 12, 2019 from: https://www.thefamouspeople.com/profiles/mao-zedong-56.php

[xx] Will Nicoll, Hoxha's pyjamas now houses a pro-democracy radio station, 30 May 2015, Retrieved April 12, 2019, from: https://www.spectator.co.uk/2015/05/the-museum-which-once- displayed-enver-hoxhas-pyjamas-now-houses-a-pro-democracy- radio-station/

[xxi] Alexandra Nicola, Interesting Facts About Nicolae Ceausescu, the Romanian Dictator, Retrieved April 12, 2019, from: https://travelmakertours.com/interesting-facts-about-nicolae- ceausescu-the-romanian-dictator/

[xxii] Giles Foden, My brutal muse, 24 Jul 2003, Retrieved April 12, 2019 from: https://www.theguardian.com/books/2003/jul/24/fiction.gilesfoden

[xxiii] Mac Prince, Of Course This Mercedes 600 Pullman Carried a Controversial Dictator, 5 Nov 2016, Retrieved April 12, 2019, from: https://www.thedrive.com/vintage/5880/of-course-this-mercedes- 600-pullman-carried-a-controversial-dictator

[xxiv] Alen Beganovic, How did Tito's foreign policies of Yugoslavia influence the politics and events of the Cold War?, November 2004, Retrieved April 12, 2019 from:

http://www.ctevans.net/Nvcc/HIS135/Events/Tito80/Tito80.html
[xxv] BIOGRAPHY, Rafael Trujillo Biography, Retrieved April 12, 2019, from: https://www.biography.com/people/rafael-trujillo-39891
[xxvi] Before They Were Despots: Dictators and Their Old Jobs, February 2, 2007, Retrieved April 12, 2019, from: https://www.neatorama.com/2007/02/02/before-they-were-despots- dictators-and-their-old-jobs/
[xxvii] Blake Stilwell, The 9 day jobs of brutal dictators, Jan. 12, 2016, Retrieved April 12, 2019 from: https://www.wearethemighty.com/articles/the-9-day-jobs-of-brutal- dictators
[xxviii] Mark Van Vugt, 7 Steps to Becoming a Dictator, Feb 05, 2017, Retrieved April 12, 2019, from: https://www.psychologytoday.com/us/blog/naturally- selected/201702/7-steps-becoming-dictator
[xxix] Tyrannical Dictators—Rule of One!, January 19, 2018, Retrieved April 12, 2019, from: https://discover.hubpages.com/education/Dictators-Rule-of-One
[xxx] Mark Harrison, The Dictator and Defense, Retrieved April 12, 2019, from: http://citeseerx.ist.psu.edu/viewdoc/download?doi=10.1.1.517.9781 &rep=rep1&type=pdf

[xxxi] Will Englund, Why Trump's 'enemy of the people' bluster can't be compared to Stalin's savage rule, January 17, 2018, Retrieved April 12, 2019 from: https://www.washingtonpost.com/news/retropolis/wp/2018/01/16/why-trumps-enemy-of-the-people-bluster-cant-be-compared-to-stalins-rule/?noredirect=on&utm_term=.a2561bf2a814

[xxxii] Wikipedia, List of Political slogans, Retrieved April 12, 2019, from: https://en.wikipedia.org/wiki/List_of_political_slogans

[xxxiii] Mark Van Vugt, 7 Steps to Becoming a Dictator, Feb 05, 2017, Retrieved April 12, 2019, from: https://www.psychologytoday.com/us/blog/naturally-selected/201702/7-steps-becoming-dictator

[xxxiv] Professor Ringen's Blog, Dictatorship and Ideology, APRIL 19, 2018, Retrieved April 12, 2019, from: https://thatsdemocracy.com/2018/04/19/dictatorship-and-ideology/

[xxxv] Mark Van Vugt, 7 Steps to Becoming a Dictator, Feb 05, 2017, Retrieved April 12, 2019, from: https://www.psychologytoday.com/us/blog/naturally-selected/201702/7-steps-becoming-dictator

[xxxvi] Sergei Guriev and Daniel Treisman, How Modern Dictators Survive: An Informational Theory of the New Authoritarianism, November 2015, Retrieved April 12, 2019, from: https://www.eui.eu/Documents/Departments Centres/Economics/Se minarsevents/Guriev-Micro.pdf

[xxxvii] Mark Van Vugt, 7 Steps to Becoming a Dictator, Feb 05, 2017, Retrieved April 12, 2019, from: https://www.psychologytoday.com/us/blog/naturally- selected/201702/7-steps-becoming-dictator

[xxxviii] Sergei Guriev and Daniel Treisman, How Modern Dictators Survive: An Informational Theory of the New Authoritarianism, November 2015, Retrieved April 12, 2019, from: https://www.eui.eu/Documents/Departments Centres/Economics/Se minarsevents/Guriev-Micro.pdf

[xxxix] The International Forum for Democratic Studies, Media Manipulation, Retrieved April 12, 2019, from: https://www.resurgentdictatorship.org/authoritarian- tactics/manipulating-media/

[xl] This Investigation is Available at his website: cicune.org

[xli] Hong Kong Free Press, China's high-tech censorship and surveillance tools are inspiring other countries, study says, 1 November 2018,

Retrieved April 12, 2019, from: https://www.hongkongfp.com/2018/11/01/chinas-high-tech- censorship-surveillance-tools-inspiring-countries-study-says/

[xlii] Richard Fontaine & Kara Frederick, The Autocrat's New Tool Kit, The Wall Street Journal, Saturday/Sunday, March 16-17, 2019, C1

[xliii] I refer to those who cannot send their families abroad, because do not have the privileges of the "Bolivarian Elite" integrated by the Cabello Rondon, Jorge Rodriguez, Chavez Frias, Rafael Ramirez, Maduro Flores between other Gangs attached to the Bolivarian Dictatorship

[xliv] Venezuela 2017 Human Rights Report, Retrieved November 04, 2018, from: https://www.justice.gov/eoir/page/file/1057096/download

[xlv] Amnesty International, Amnesty International Report 2017/18, Retrieved November 04, 2018, from: https://www.justice.gov/sites/default/files/pages/attachments/2018/03/06/ai_2018.pdf#page=393

[xlvi] Human Right Watch, Country Summary: Venezuela, (January 2018), Retrieved November 04, 2018, from: https://www.justice.gov/eoir/page/file/1043001/download

[xlvii] Sebastiana Barraez, The enigma of military assassinations in Venezuela, March 21, 2017, Retrieved April 12, 2019, from: http://elestimulo.com/blog/el-enigma-de-los-asesinatos-de- militares-en-venezuela/

[xlviii] Sebastiana Barraez, Sebastiana Barraez: La lista de los 152 Militares detenidos en Venezuela accused of Treason, Apr 8, 2019, Retrieved April 12, 2019 from: https://puntodecorte.com/sebastiana-barraez-lista-militares- detenidos/

www.ingramcontent.com/pod-product-compliance
Lightning Source LLC
LaVergne TN
LVHW051038070526
838201LV00066B/4846